Aural Tests in Mathematics

BOOK 5

Wyvern Project Group

Christopher Gardner (Project Leader)
Norman Baker
Keith Jackson
Vernon Mortimer
Barbara Roberts
Jenny Schofield
John Suik
Pam Gahame

John Murray

© Wyvern Project Group 1989

First published in 1989 by
John Murray (Publishers) Ltd,
50 Albemarle Street, London W1X 4BD

Text and cover design by Tony Stocks

Printed in Great Britain
by St Edmundsbury Press

British Library Cataloguing in Publication Data

Aural tests in mathematics.
  1. Mathematics – Questions & Answers –
  For schools
  I. Wyvern Project Group
  510′.76

ISBN 0-7195-4592-7 Bk. 5

ISBN 0-7195-4588-9 Bk. 1
ISBN 0-7195-4589-7 Bk. 2
ISBN 0-7195-4590-0 Bk. 3
ISBN 0-7195-4591-0 Bk. 4

Introduction

Recent research and reports on children's understanding of mathematics, particularly the Cockcroft Report, 'Mathematics Counts', have stressed the importance of mental aptitudes in mathematics. Aural tests, such as those presented in this series, are one very effective means of improving children's performance in this important area.

The tests presented here, and in other books in this series, are the product of several years of trials. They are designed for ease of administration and to form a regular part of any course leading to GCSE, Standard Grade or equivalent qualification. Used in any course, they will help children to think quickly and to use their mathematical abilities in a wide range of everyday situations. For some examining bodies, tests of this type form part of the final assessment, so preparation for this style of testing is additionally useful.

The Tests

All tests have fifteen questions. In this book the first seven contain material from areas common to school courses for a particular age group. The remaining eight questions are based on matter found in advertisements, newspapers etc. and which is provided in copiable form. They require pupils to use their mathematical skills to solve a wide range of everyday problems.

Each book contains enough material so that pupils can have one test per week throughout the normal school year.

Book 1 has seven topic-related tests, designed for level differentiation, thirty tests at level 1 and thirty tests at level 2.
Books 2 and 3 each have thirty tests at both levels 1 and 2.
Book 4 has thirty tests at GCSE levels 1, 2 and 3.
Book 5 has twenty-five tests and five extension tests, at levels 1, 2 and 3.

Using Aural Tests

Although our testing has been quite extensive, we are aware that it is not possible to match the coursework element with that of every school. Thus teachers may find it worthwhile to modify some of the questions (and answers).

For each test, there is

- a set of questions and answers
- a students' information sheet (a common sheet for all 3 levels).

All the material which makes up the tests is provided with a copyright waiver so that class sets of the information sheets and several sets of the questions and answers can be produced. For ourselves, and in some of the trials schools, we have found it worthwhile to make up pupils' booklets for each year group.

The standard pattern of administration we have used is as follows:

1 Teacher circulates information sheets (or booklets), plus paper to record answers and make notes.
2 Each question is read out **twice**, in a continuous manner, emphasising key words. Pupils are advised to take down relevant facts, but after a few weeks' practice they should not be allowed to ask questions during the test.
3 There is a period of silence for pupils to do the necessary recording and circulation. The gap between questions is not regulated at this stage, but most pupils finish (if capable of doing so) within 15 to 30 seconds.
4 Answer sheets (or books) are exchanged after the test has been completed.
5 Teacher reads out the answers, and scores are recorded.

The whole process normally takes about twenty minutes, although with related (and often very useful) discussion one test can often take up a much longer period.

Pupils' Attitudes

Nothing is more likely to succeed than evidence of success. Thus the questions in each test have been designed so that most pupils will achieve at least a 50% score. Additionally, within each set of tests for a year group, we have tried to adjust the difficulty gradient so that pupils are aware of their improving competence. Pupils who have objective evidence of steady improvement are, in our experience, more positively motivated. This is very much more desirable than the situation where lower achievers make overly harsh judgements about themselves in relation to their peers.

Question and Answer Sheets

30 tests : GCSE level 1 — lower
GCSE level 2 — intermediate
GCSE level 3 — higher

Test 1

1 What would be the cost of buying five shirts at eight pounds each?

2 How many minutes are there in two and a quarter hours?

3 Write down all the factors of fourteen.

4 What would be the average speed of a car which travels forty-eight kilometres in half an hour?

5 Find the cost of a meal which costs forty pounds plus VAT at fifteen per cent.

6 If I bought a box of chocolates for two pounds forty-six pence with a five pound note, how much change would I get?

7 How many degrees do the three angles of a triangle add up to?

You will now need your Information Sheet

8 Estimate the size of the angle marked in the triangle.

9 If the shop opens every day at nine a.m., how many hours is it open for on Tuesday?

10 How much do you save by buying this box of cereals now?

11 How long does the fifteen fifty-eight train from Bethnal Green take to get to Lower Edmonton?

12 How much will the car cost you in total using this loan?

13 How much extra would you have to pay for a one point four S Fiesta rather than a one point one L Fiesta at the normal price?

14 How much extra a week will it cost to borrow four thousand pounds for thirty-six months rather than fifteen hundred pounds over the same period?

15 How much would it cost to buy a house worth fifty thousand pounds, if the price increases at the same rate?

ANSWERS

1 £40	6 £2.54	11 21 min
2 135	7 180°	12 £7367.40
3 1,2,7,14	8 20–40°	13 £623
4 96 km/h	9 11 h	14 £20.68
5 £46	10 12p	15 £250

Test 2

1 Ninety-six apprentices took a trade test. One quarter of them passed with grade A marks. How many of them received grade A?

2 Two hundred and thirty-eight people went to a disco. By eleven-thirty only eighty-nine remained. How many had left?

3 *Girl Magazine* costs thirty-eight pence. Shirley buys nine copies. How much change does she get from a five pound note?

4 My train left at eight thirty-seven a.m. and it arrived at its destination at nine minutes past two in the afternoon. In hours and minutes how long did the journey take?

5 Write two thousand and seven and three-quarters as a decimal number.

6 On a clock the minute hand moves much faster than the hour hand. How many times as fast does it move?

7 There are twenty-seven bindas to the English pound in the country of Lendow. How many bindas will I get for twenty pounds?

You will now need your Information Sheet

8 How much change will I get from one thousand pounds if I pay the room price?

9 What is the numerical difference between the temperature in degrees Celsius in Frankfurt and degrees Fahrenheit in Frankfurt?

10 What is the cost of a nine day coach holiday for a family of six?

11 George pays four pounds and six pence for packs of apples. How many packs does he buy?

12 By how much does the profit before taxation in nineteen eighty-seven exceed that in nineteen eighty-six?

13 The number of countries in which BP has employees will increase next year by ten per cent. What will that bring the total to?

14 What is the perimeter of one of the fields owned by the brothers?

15 Write in words the price of the Vitesse.

ANSWERS

1 24	6 12	11 14
2 149	7 540	12 £59 m
3 £1.58	8 £23.25	13 77
4 5 h 32 min	9 47	14 2 miles
5 2007.75	10 £954	15 Nine thousand, three hundred and forty-three pounds

Test 3

1 What factors are common to forty-two and forty-nine?

2 A regular polygon has an interior angle of sixty degrees. How many sides does it have?

3 What is the decimal value of the square of one-half?

4 How long will a journey of one hundred and eighty kilometres take when averaging forty kilometres per hour?

5 How many minutes are there between ten twenty-seven and fourteen thirty-six?

6 A number written in standard form is six point six times ten to the four. Write this number in figures.

7 Taking pi as three, work out the area of a circle of radius two centimetres.

You will now need your Information Sheet

8 What is the cost of tickets for two children and two adults for Boxing-day?

9 For how many hours is the pitch available on Sunday?

10 What was the price of platinum at the end of May?

11 What is the total cost of a hi-fi cabinet and a TV cabinet?

12 What is the difference in the percentage figure for insurance in nineteen eighty-five and in nineteen eighty-six?

13 Write in figures the numbers of scientists doing pure research in nineteen seventy-seven.

14 How many employees were working for this firm in nineteen eight-five/eighty-six?

15 What is the approximate percentage reduction on a nine-carat gold St. Christopher?

ANSWERS

1	7	6	66 000	11	£298
2	3	7	12 cm^2	12	1.4%
3	0.25	8	£18	13	27 000 –
4	4.5 h	9	4.5 h		33 000
5	249	10	£570 – £580	14	131 466
				15	50%

Test 4

1 Helen is saving up to buy a pair of shoes which costs twenty-two pounds fifty pence. She saves two pounds fifty pence a week. How long will it take her to save enough to buy the shoes?

2 Three shepherds each looked after twelve sheep in a competition to find the champion sheep. How many legs did all the shepherds and all the sheep have when totalled up?

3 A man is training for a marathon race. For five days he goes for a seven mile run. For the next five days he doubles that. How many miles has he run altogether during these ten days?

4 By how many is four hundred and sixty-eight less than one thousand nine hundred and thirty-seven?

5 A race horse ran in sixty races. It won twenty-four times. What percentage of winning races is this?

6 A patient has to take two tablets every six hours. How many tablets will he take in a week?

7 There were thirteen pictures for auction. The total money received for them was one thousand, nine hundred and fifty pounds. What was the average amount paid for each picture?

You will now need your Information Sheet

8 How much more would you pay for two gold chains than for two sets of gold earrings?

9 In hours, minutes and seconds, how much less time did Jeff Rees take to run the marathon than Sarah Ayling?

10 In his first year the warehouse manager was given bonuses of one tenth of his annual salary. How much did he receive in salary and bonuses?

11 Amanda had saved one hundred and fifty pounds. After buying a single quilt from the Co-op and a king-sized quilt from House of Fraser, how much did she have left?

12 How many tons of feed would Egg City's layers need for a fortnight?

13 I change five pounds of money into Belgian francs. How many francs do I get?

14 Seven royal albatrosses each lay an egg. How many total days of incubation altogether elapse before the eggs hatch?

15 Six gardeners are responsible for maintaining the grounds and gardens at Osborne House. The work is shared equally. How many acres is each gardener responsible for?

ANSWERS

1	9 weeks	6	56	11	£30.06
2	150	7	£150	12	3500 tons
3	105 miles	8	£9.70	13	307.25 BF
4	1469	9	1 h 15 min 36 s	14	546
5	40%	10	£8250	15	75 acres

Test 5

1 What is the average (mean) of the following temperatures: minus one degree, zero degrees, one degree, minus three degrees and two degrees?

2 Point six of the class are aged between eleven and a half and twelve. If this information is transferred to a pie chart, what will be the angle of the sector representing this age group?

3 Estimate the square root of one thousand, two hundred and ten.

4 A right-angled triangle has a hypotenuse of thirteen centimetres and one other side of twelve centimetres. What is the area of the triangle?

5 What is the area of the net of a wedge which has as its cross-section a right-angled triangle of base four centimetres and height three centimetres? The width of the wedge is six centimetres.

6 Carpet squares are advertised as being one metre square correct to the nearest centimetre. What is the difference in area between the largest and smallest size the squares could be? Give your answer in square centimetres.

7 A home worker is paid one pound per hour plus two pence per article produced. How much is she paid for an hour in which she makes seventy-six articles?

You will now need your Information Sheet

8 The exchange rate is one pound for nine point five French francs. Give an estimate of the sterling equivalent of this French supermarket bill.

9 Write in decimal figures the maximum value for the expansion coefficient at four hundred degrees K.

10 Which number occurs most often as a prime factor of these numbers?

11 Discount is taken off before VAT at fifteen per cent is added. How much will I pay for kitchen units which originally cost one thousand, nine hundred pounds?

12 I bought the Y registered Honda fifty for twenty-four payments of fifteen pounds. How much more than the cash price did I pay in total?

13 How much do five, new seven hundred by fifteen eight-ply tyres cost?

14 Write down the amount spent in each of the two years when there was no change.

15 Use your ruler to find out the height of the shuttle train's roof above the track. Give your answer in metres.

ANSWERS

1 −0.2°	6 400 cm²	11 £1667.50
2 216°	7 £2.52	12 £85
3 34–36	8 £27–£29	13 £199.50
4 30 cm²	9 0.000007–	14 £5 100 000
5 84 cm²	0.0000065 K⁻¹	15 5.4–5.5 m
	10 2	

Test 6

1 What is the difference between three hundred and ten and one hundred and fifty-eight?

2 Write forty thousand and three in figures.

3 In a factory, a worker produces a part of a washing machine in eighteen minutes. How long, in hours and minutes, will it take to produce eleven parts?

4 You earn three pounds an hour. Your employer gives you a twenty per cent rise. How much an hour do you now earn?

5 Two angles of a triangle measure fifty-five degrees and sixty degrees. What does the other angle measure?

6 Find the value of the following: six y divided by x, if x equals four and y equals six.

7 You cut a pack of playing cards. What is the probability of you cutting a nine? Give your answer in the form of one in however many.

You will now need your Information Sheet

8 You buy five pounds of whole gammon. How much do you pay?

9 On the Ansett Pioneers' national coach network you average two hundred miles a day. How many miles do you cover in the time stated for a cost of about one hundred and fifty pounds?

10 On the list shown what is the difference in degrees Fahrenheit between the coldest place and the hottest place?

11 At the price shown what, to the nearest pound, would fifteen volumes of the children's Britannica cost?

12 Sixty-three people go on the British coach tour. How many of them pay?

13 The church in Andernach is a tourist attraction. To the nearest fifty years, how long ago was it built, assuming that it was built in the second half of the thirteenth century?

14 Estimate in centimetres the length of the line.

15 In nineteen sixty-eight you bought one prescription a week at two shillings and six old pence each for six weeks. How much does that work out at altogether in the currency we now use, given that one shilling equals five new pence and there were twelve old pence to the shilling?

ANSWERS

1 152	6 9	11 £60
2 40 003	7 1 in 13	12 56
3 3 h 18 min	8 £4.40	13 700 years
4 £3.60	9 3 000 miles	14 7–11 cm
5 65°	10 23°F	15 75p

Test 7

1 A swimming pool is fifty metres long. How many lengths does Jenny have to swim in order to cover a distance of one kilometre?

2 How much interest is earned when four hundred pounds is invested for one year at eight per cent interest rate?

3 What is the perimeter of a rectangular field which is four hundred and fifty metres long and two hundred and ten metres wide?

4 A unit of electricity costs four and a half pence. How many units can be bought for one pound eighty pence?

5 What is the nearest prime number to thirty-three?

6 Which of the following is a quadrilateral: isosceles triangle, circle, parallelogram, hexagon or pentagon?

7 What is the mean of sixty pence, two pounds, one pound twenty pence and twenty pence?

You will now need your Information Sheet

8 How much does the pack of yogurts weigh?

9 Estimate the three figure heading of Haworth from Lumbfoot.

10 How many arcs has this network?

11 How much would a thousand units have cost in eighty-six stroke seven, giving your answer in pounds and pence?

12 What would the monthly income for an investment of one thousand pounds be?

13 What is the size of the angle marked a?

14 Which of these letters have just one line of symmetry?

15 What was the maximum difference in temperature in degrees Fahrenheit?

ANSWERS

1 20	6 Parallelogram	11 £19.03
2 £32	7 £1	12 £8.75
3 1320 m	8 1500 g	13 108°
4 40	9 100°–115°	14 D and W
5 31	10 4	15 52°F

Test 8

1 Write the number seventeen point six five correct to two significant figures.

2 The average (mean) of three numbers is five. Two of the numbers are two and six. What is the third?

3 Write four-fifths as a decimal fraction.

4 I buy pens at two pounds for twenty. I make twenty per cent profit. For how much do I sell each pen?

5 Give the y co-ordinates of the point which lies on the line y equals two x plus one, which has an x co-ordinate of two.

6 A bicycle wheel has a radius of thirty centimetres. Taking pi as three, give the approximate distance the bicycle travels forward in one revolution of the wheel.

7 What is the direction I must travel in to return home after an outward journey on a bearing nought seven five degrees?

You will now need your Information Sheet

8 What is the price of two single convector radiators, fifty point four inches long?

9 What is the cost of one bottle of Evian water, two glasses of Coca Cola and some peanuts? The prices are in sterling.

10 What was the original price of the Amstrad four six nought nought video?

11 What is the time taken for the trip to Ilfracombe from Portishead on August the first?

12 What is the cost of twelve metres of fifteen millimetre copper tube?

13 What was the inflation rate mid-way through nineteen eighty-seven?

14 What is the total cost of two, one hundred and eighty-five stroke sixty HR fourteen tyres including VAT?

15 How much is saved by buying fifty contractors' wheelbarrows?

ANSWERS

1 18	6 180 cm	11 10 h 40 min
2 7	7 255°	12 £8.76
3 0.8	8 £50.16	13 4.1–4.3%
4 12p	9 £1.80	14 £87.40
5 5	10 £329.99	15 £150

Test 9

1 What is the sum of two point five and nought point six?
2 Write three-fifths as a decimal.
3 When two coins are tossed what is the probability of getting two heads?
4 Write five to ten at night in twenty-four-hour-clock time.
5 What is the inverse of divide by five?
6 How many lines of symmetry has a rectangle?
7 How many metres in two point three kilometres?

You will now need your Information Sheet

8 A party of people attend on Friday the tenth and are charged seventy-two pounds. How many people are in the party?
9 Which of these letters has just one line of symmetry?
10 Estimate the three figure bearing of Reading from Oxford.
11 How much VAT is payable on the garage price?
12 Write the nineteen eighty-seven group turnover in figures.
13 The scale of this map is one centimetre to one kilometre. Estimate the real length of Devonshire Road.
14 An offer of eighty-nine thousand, two hundred pounds is made on this house. How much less than the asking price is this?
15 How much would a bed priced at eighty-four pounds cost in this sale?

ANSWERS

1 3.1	6 2	11 £480
2 0.6	7 2300 m	12 4 220 800 000
3 $\frac{1}{4}$	8 24	13 2.3 – 2.5 km
4 21 55	9 M	14 £5800
5 Multiply by five	10 150° – 160°	15 £63

Test 10

1 A motorist travels twenty-two miles in fifteen minutes. What is his average speed?
2 In a class of thirty children two-fifths are boys. How many boys are there in the class?
3 David receives fifty pence change from a five pound note after buying three records all at the same price. How much was each record?
4 The perimeter of a square is twenty centimetres. What is the area of the square?
5 The sun rises at four twenty-seven a.m. and sets at nine thirty-four p.m. How many hours and minutes of daylight are there?
6 Green paint is made from yellow and blue paint in the ratio of two to three. How much yellow paint is used to make twenty litres of green paint?
7 How many lines of symmetry does an isosceles triangle have?

You will now need your Information Sheet

8 How many pounds would four cans of corned beef weigh?
9 What was the height of the tide on Monday evening?
10 What is the area of this triangle?
11 What is the weekly repayment for a seven thousand pound loan over five years?
12 How much would a window frame normally priced at eighty pounds cost?
13 What is the size of angle a?
14 How much does one A-four leaflet cost?
15 What is the three figure bearing of B from A?

ANSWERS

1 88 m.p.h.	6 8 litres	11 £38.83
2 12	7 1	12 £60
3 £1.50	8 3	13 30°
4 25 cm²	9 13.7 m	14 1.5p
5 17 h 7 min	10 24 cm²	15 100° – 110°

Test 11

1 A shopkeeper buys radios for fifteen pounds and sells them at a profit of twenty per cent. What is the selling price?

2 John divides his bar of chocolate and eats half today. Tomorrow he will eat a quarter of what he has left. What fraction of the whole bar will he eat tomorrow?

3 A motor cycle advertised for one thousand, five hundred and fifty pounds can be bought on hire purchase for a ten per cent deposit and twenty-four monthly payments of eighty pounds. How much is the deposit?

4 Write the number seventy point three six correct to three significant figures.

5 Write down the factors of twelve.

6 A piece of wire thirty-six centimetres long is bent, and cut where necessary, to form the edges of a cube. How long is each edge?

7 Twelve apples cost sixty pence, how much do fifteen cost?

You will now need your Information Sheet

8 How many British resorts were warmer than Amsterdam?

9 What is the cost of four fourteen inch cheese and tomato pizzas?

10 How many fewer railway staff were employed at the end of this period than in nineteen eighty-two?

11 What is the total amount paid back each year on a loan of two thousand pounds borrowed for three years?

12 The ferry time is quoted to the nearest hour. What is the biggest possible difference between the ferry and the Eurotunnel?

13 In nineteen eighty-four one part of the world accounted for just over half the world's population. Where was that?

14 What was the total number of minutes spent on yachting?

15 What is the cost excluding VAT of a short advert taking two lines?

ANSWERS

1 £18	6 3 cm	11 £860.08
2 $\frac{1}{8}$	7 75p	12 4.5 h
3 £155	8 9	13 Asia
4 70.4	9 £13	14 1000 min
5 1,2,3,4,6,12	10 10 000–20 000	15 £28.50

Test 12

1 How many circular discs of diameter two centimetres can be cut from a piece of metal fourteen centimetres by ten centimetres?

2 How much time remains on a three hour cassette after recording programmes of one hour twenty minutes and one and a quarter hours duration?

3 Seventeen sweets weigh two hundred grams. How many similar sweets weigh one kilogram?

4 How long would it take a motorist averaging eighty kilometres an hour to travel sixty kilometres?

5 Mr Williams' hourly overtime pay of one and a half times his normal hourly rate is three pounds. What is his normal hourly rate?

6 What is the difference between negative six and positive twelve?

7 Five-eighths of the pupils in a school are girls. What fraction of the pupils are boys?

You will now need your Information Sheet

8 How much does the pack of crisps weigh?

9 Write the eighty-five stroke six sales of units in figures.

10 What is the difference between the Fiesta and Escort monthly hire charges, including VAT?

11 How many French francs will ten pounds buy?

12 Estimate the perimeter of this rectangle in centimetres.

13 How much is saved on a three pound shoulder of lamb?

14 Estimate the three figure bearing of Bath from Bristol.

15 What is the size of the angle marked a?

ANSWERS

1 35	6 18	11 97.4 FF
2 25 min	7 $\frac{3}{8}$	12 12–16 cm
3 85	8 175 g	13 39p
4 45 min	9 227 000 000 000 units	14 110°–120°
5 £2	10 £24.96	15 80°

Test 13

1 Darren buys five rulers and receives seventy pence change from two pounds. How much was each ruler?

2 A triangle has an area of twelve square centimetres. The height of the triangle is four centimetres. What is the length of its base?

3 What is the square of a half?

4 Express four-fifths as a decimal.

5 Three angles of a quadrilateral are all seventy degrees. What is the size of the fourth angle?

6 At five a.m. the temperature was minus nine degrees centigrade, by noon the temperature had risen by twenty-one degrees. What was the noon temperature?

7 List the prime factors of twenty.

You will now need your Information Sheet

8 How much is saved on the Stonehill Bureau unit?

9 Write this figure to the nearest thousand.

10 Estimate the three figure bearing of Southend from Reading.

11 Give the co-ordinates of A after a reflection in the x-axis.

12 Which of these letters have no lines of symmetry?

13 On which day did the highest tide occur?

14 Express this reduction as a fraction.

15 Calculate angle a.

ANSWERS

1 26p	6 12°C	11 $(-3, 1)$
2 6cm	7 2 and 5	12 N, S
3 $\frac{1}{4}$	8 £59.50	13 Wednesday
4 0.8	9 874000	14 $\frac{1}{5}$
5 150°	10 80°–90°	15 40°

Test 14

1 How many sweets will thirty pupils have between them if on average they have fifteen each?

2 Four friends share out eight hundred and eight marbles equally between themselves. How many do they each get?

3 You increase eighty-eight by nineteen. How many have you?

4 Write seven point five as a whole number and a fraction.

5 A lawn is fourteen yards long and twelve yards wide. What is the area of the lawn?

6 Ross is sixteen years old. In two years time he will be twice as old as his brother Mike. How old is Mike?

7 What is four per cent of six hundred and fifty pounds?

You will now need your Information Sheet

8 Estimate the number of tourists in the USA during nineteen eighty-two.

9 How many people work in Hong Kong if one hundred thousand people work in either agriculture or fishing?

10 What size of electorate was most frequent in English boroughs in the eighteenth century?

11 How much will it cost me in total for the BMW twins with a round filter and an oil cooler if I need a BMW carb service kit as well?

12 This advertisement appeared in nineteen eighty-five, exactly four years after the machine had been made. What was its average mileage per year to the nearest mile?

13 How many people are employed along the Fraser?

14 At this time there were an equal number of women and men in Tibet. How many women were there?

15 How much will it cost me to buy the goggles and reflective safety belt?

ANSWERS

1 450	6 7	11 £30.90
2 202	7 £26	12 6737
3 107	8 1.5 million	13 8500
4 $7\frac{1}{2}$	9 10 million	14 480 000
5 168 yard²	10 Under 500	15 £21.35

Test 15

1 For protection against freezing in the winter the mixture in the car radiator should be twenty-five per cent antifreeze. How much antifreeze will I need for my car which has a seventeen pint cooling system?

2 I measure my room as fourteen feet three inches by eight feet two inches. What is the approximate number of square yards of carpet needed?

3 A long playing record revolves thirty-three and one-third times per minute. How many times does it go round during the playing of a five minute song?

4 What is the nearest whole number to the square root of one hundred and sixty?

5 A calculator display shows three point six then a gap then five. Write this answer as a single number.

6 Last night the temperature was minus three degrees. That was four degrees colder than the previous night. What was the temperature then?

7 What is the interior angle of a regular three-sided polygon?

You will now need your Information Sheet

8 What is the saving on buying two new five hundred and seventy-six page account books?

9 How many months would it take to pay back the purchase price of the most expensive midi hi-fi with compact disc?

10 How long does it take the bus to get from The Heron at Locking Road to Wells?

11 How many deutschmarks could be obtained for a dollar at the end of June?

12 How much could a worker in a UK owned engineering company expect to earn in a year?

13 The exchange rate is one pound for nine point five French francs. Approximately, what was the equivalent price of the total bill?

14 Loft insulation costs two hundred pounds, how many years would it take to recover that money if you were using gas fuel?

15 How much interest would I earn in one year on three thousand pounds?

ANSWERS
1 4.25 pints	6 1°	11 1.82–1.84 DM
2 13–17 yard²	7 60°	12 £8000–£9000
3 166⅔	8 £74.12	13 £3.20–£3.60
4 13	9 24	14 5 years
5 360000	10 52 min	15 £210

Test 16

1 A triangle with a height of eight centimetres has an area of thirty-two square centimetres. What is the length of the triangle's base?

2 A bottle contains a quarter of a litre of medicine. The patient must take ten five-millilitre doses of medicine a day. For how long will the medicine last?

3 In a class one-third are boys, of these a half are fair-haired. What fraction of the class is made up of fair-haired boys?

4 How much time remains on a three hour video cassette after a film of one hundred and fifteen minutes duration has been recorded?

5 Write down all the prime numbers between twenty-five and thirty.

6 In a test Ahmed scored eleven out of twenty. What percentage is this?

7 Write the number twenty-four thousand and seven in figures.

You will now need your Information Sheet

8 How much would it cost to carpet a room measuring six yards by five yards using the cheapest carpet?

9 Express the reduction for the first customer as a fully simplified fraction.

10 What is the difference between the highest and lowest thermal efficiencies?

11 The test fee is an extra ten per cent. How much is this?

12 How much heavier was Tucker than Tyson?

13 A thirty-eight year old man chooses plan B. How much will he have to pay each month?

14 To the nearest penny, how much does each slice cost?

15 What type of triangle is this?

ANSWERS
1 8 cm	6 55%	11 £26.50
2 5 days	7 24007	12 6 lb
3 ⅙	8 £179.70	13 £8.40
4 65 min	9 7/10	14 10p
5 29	10 1.03%	15 Isosceles

Test 17

1 A triangle with a height of eleven centimetres has an area of forty-four square centimetres. What is the length of its base?

2 Which three consecutive numbers have a sum of twenty-one?

3 On an activities afternoon half the class have gone ice skating and one-third have gone ten pin bowling. The rest have gone swimming. What fraction of the class have gone swimming?

4 Which prime numbers are between twenty and thirty?

5 Justine and Mary share twenty sweets in the ratio of two to three. How many more sweets does Mary get than Justine?

6 Give the next number in this series: one, two, four, seven.

7 At five a.m. the temperature in Helsinki is minus fifteen degrees. By nine a.m. it has risen by six degrees. What is the nine a.m. temperature?

You will now need your Information Sheet

8 The credit terms are for two years. What is the credit price?

9 The figures in heavy black type are the number of goals scored so far this season by these teams. How many goals were scored altogether in this division?

10 What is the ratio of Cantonese to Chaozhou people in Hong Kong?

11 Estimate the distance from Freeport to Nassau.

12 How much of Hong Kong's invisible trade in nineteen seventy-eight was due to transportation?

13 How much would a fourteen night holiday in Tenerife cost for two people?

14 What is the size of the angle marked a?

15 What was the index value for food production in nineteen sixty?

ANSWERS

1	8cm	6	11	11	150–200 km
2	6,7,8	7	−9°	12	8000–9000 m
3	$\frac{1}{6}$	8	£264	13	£498
4	23 and 29	9	17	14	105°
5	4	10	6:1	15	120–123

Test 18

1 How many circular patches of radius three point seven five centimetres can be cut from a square piece of material with sides of forty centimetres?

2 What decimal fraction is equivalent to three-fifths?

3 When using a calculator to multiply one point five by seven point two five the string of numbers, one zero eight seven five is obtained. Put the decimal point in the correct position.

4 The distance measured between two points is five hundred and thirty metres correct to the nearest metre. What is the smallest distance it could be?

5 What is the cube root of eight?

6 Write down the smallest number which is a multiple of seven and eleven.

7 A man averages five kilometres an hour when walking. How far can he walk in six and a half hours?

You will now need your Information Sheet

8 In nineteen eighty-three when was it expected that silver would run out?

9 I paid ten per cent deposit on the DL manual estate, how much is left to pay?

10 Estimate the distance from Murra to the Hunza.

11 Which microcomputer was the modal machine?

12 What would be the cost of four, one nine five stroke fifty VR times fifteens?

13 What is the cost to the nearest pound of three single divans?

14 What do the thirty-six monthly payments of eighty-two pounds twenty-four pence equal?

15 What is the cost of one black plastic refuse sack if I bought in a lot of one thousand?

ANSWERS

1	25	6	77	11	RML 380Z
2	0.6	7	32.5 km	12	£247
3	10.875	8	2006–2007	13	£120
4	529.5 m	9	£5125.50	14	£2960.64
5	2	10	180–220 miles	15	4.5p

Test 19

1 Peter walked thirty miles in a sponsored event. He took eight hours to complete the walk. How many miles an hour was he walking?
2 Jodie bought seventeen badges for five pounds and ten pence. How much did each badge cost?
3 In a small factory there were one hundred and ninety-eight workers. For every two women there were seven men. How many of each were there?
4 In a large comprehensive school three hundred and fifty people took a mock examination in mathematics. Only sixteen per cent of them passed at the highest level. How many passed at lower levels?
5 *l* equals six, *y* equals eight, *z* equals four. What is two *y* multiplied by *z* minus three *l* ?
6 When visiting America Paula needed to change some English money into dollars, the exchange rate was one point six dollars to the pound. How many dollars would she get for thirty pounds?
7 In a golf tournament the winner had rounds of seventy, sixty-six, sixty-eight and sixty-seven. What was the average number of strokes he took for each round?

You will now need your Information Sheet

8 Write the number in the first line of this story in figures.
9 What is the perimeter (all the way round) of one of the front mats?
10 The sandwich tins hold twenty sandwiches. One is full, the other is four-fifths full. How many more sandwiches will be needed to have them both full?
11 Eight people in a family pay equal shares into the minimum investment. How much does each of them contribute?
12 How much will I save by buying my scented polyanthus in one lot of twenty rather than two lots of ten?
13 To the nearest five pounds how much each day will the seven day holiday in Rome cost me if I go in October?
14 Three people decide to go on the trekking holiday. They wish to each have two hundred pounds spending money. How much will they need altogether?
15 In one of their last five matches QPR won one–nil. What was the average number of goals they conceded in each of the other matches?

ANSWERS

1 3.75 m.p.h.	6 48	11 £1250
2 30p	7 67.75	12 £1.95
3 44 women,	8 3 000 000	13 £45
154 men	9 90 inches	14 £1650
4 294	10 4	15 4.5
5 46		

Test 20

1 Jane buys three rolls at fifteen pence each and a cup of coffee. Her bill is seventy pence. How much did the coffee cost?
2 A bar of chocoloate is cut into halves and one half is cut into three equal pieces. What fraction of the bar is one of the smaller pieces?
3 Between² which two whole numbers does the square root of one hundred and sixty-five lie?
4 A cuboid is seven centimetres long, five centimetres wide and three centimetres high. What is the area of one of the largest faces?
5 I get a ten per cent discount when buying a car for cash. How much will I pay for a car listed at four thousand, seven hundred and fifty pounds?
6 An aeroplane takes three and a half hours to fly two thousand, one hundred miles. What is its average speed?
7 Solve the equation two x minus three equals five.

You will now need your Information Sheet

8 Estimate the speed at which the nine eleven Carrera changes into top gear.
9 How much would one night's camping be for two adults at the height of the season?
10 For how many hours a week is petrol available at Shepton Mallet Motors?
11 What is the saving on men's Slazenger slipovers?
12 The percentage discount has been blanked out on this advertisement. Using the Barrett Lima three piece suite to help, estimate the percentage rate.
13 I need fifteen bags of Mendip top soil. What can I expect to pay?
14 How much is saved by buying a pair of shock absorbers rather than one at a time, before VAT?
15 How many posts will I need to put up eight of the five pound ninety-five pence fencing panels?

ANSWERS

1 25p	6 600 m.p.h.	11 £4.49
2 $\frac{1}{6}$	7 x = 4	12 25%
3 12 and 13	8 121 m.p.h.	13 £13.50
4 35 cm²	9 £4.60	14 £3.30
5 £4275	10 75 h	15 9

Test 21

1 Write two-fifths as a percentage.

2 To the nearest whole number how many times will the diameter of a circle fit into its circumference?

3 A man turns thirty-two degrees anticlockwise from due west. What is his new bearing?

4 What would be the length of each side of a cube whose volume is one hundred and twenty-five cubic centimetres?

5 How many lines of symmetry has an equilateral triangle?

6 You can get twenty-three schillings in Austria for every pound sterling. How many schillings would you get for twenty pounds?

7 Write the number which is one smaller than ten thousand.

You will now need your Information Sheet

8 How much would it cost for a husband, wife and two children aged six and three, to eat a meal at this restaurant?

9 How much would it cost me to buy four and a half kilograms of lawn seed?

10 Approximately how many pupils were there in primary school in nineteen eighty-six?

11 Which cities had the hottest temperature?

12 How much do I save by paying the fleet price on a two litre SLX five door Bluebird?

13 What is the cheapest final cost of this loft insulation when VAT is added at fifteen per cent?

14 This survey asked ten thousand people; how many 'don't know' the answer in January?

15 How much do I save by buying the Vi Spring divans?

ANSWERS

1 40%	6 460	11 Moscow and
2 3	7 9999	Rhodes
3 238°	8 £15.85	12 £1218
4 5cm	9 £14.70	13 £40.25
5 3	10 3.25 million –	14 2200
	3.75 million	15 £582.50

Test 22

1 Add together the first seven odd numbers.

2 What size is each angle of an equilateral triangle?

3 What is the average (mean) of ten, eight, nine, three, seven and eleven?

4 If John shares half his chocolate bar equally between his three friends, what fraction of the whole bar does each friend get?

5 How long will it take to cook a turkey that weighs eight pounds, if you should allow twenty minutes per pound plus ten minutes to warm up the oven?

6 A plant grows two and a half centimetres every day, how long will it take to grow by one metre?

7 A train travels at an average of one hundred and twenty kilometres per hour and a coach at ninety kilometres per hour. How much longer will the coach take to go seven hundred and twenty kilometres?

You will now need your Information Sheet

8 How much will it cost you to fit your own Hunter reconditioned engine?

9 What is the saving on this machine before VAT is added?

10 How much would be paid out if a forty-four year old man died who did not smoke and paid fifteen pounds per month?

11 How many hours is this person expected to work in the day time?

12 How high is the tide expected to be on Sunday morning?

13 How much do you save by buying the three foot mattress in the sale?

14 How much will this house be worth next year if it is expected to rise by ten per cent of its value?

15 How much change would I get from ten thousand pounds if I bought ten of these three piece suites?

ANSWERS

1 49	6 40 days	11 9h 15 min
2 60°	7 2h	12 11.9 m
3 8	8 £168	13 £39
4 $\frac{1}{6}$	9 £650	14 £62 700
5 2h 50 min	10 £36 728	15 £4010

Test 23

1 What is the area of a triangle which has a base of six centimetres, perpendicular height of eight centimetres and sloping side of ten centimetres?

2 The angle at the top of an isosceles triangle is forty degrees. How many degrees each are the angles that are opposite the two sides that are equal in length?

3 How many lines of symmetry does a rectangle have?

4 What is the probability of picking a picture card, i.e. Jack, Queen or King, from an ordinary pack of playing cards?

5 What is the average speed of a car that travels thirty-four kilometres in twenty minutes?

6 An English pound is worth four and a half German marks. If I have seven pounds, how many marks could I get in exchange for them?

7 Find the mean of the first ten counting numbers.

You will now need your Information Sheet

8 How many extra hours a week is the bank open for?

9 What is the difference between the number of goals given away by Star Wanderers and Worcester College?

10 How many of the larger Riven Finish slabs will I need to cover a patio ten feet by six feet?

11 Which country has the lowest unemployment rate in this table?

12 Four people shared a house in North Oxford. How much each would they have to pay per month?

13 What is the saving on the number two size pellets?

14 How much is an egg worth according to this advert?

15 How many hours is this showroom open for at week-ends?

ANSWERS

1 24 cm^2	6 31.5 marks	11 Switzerland
2 70°	7 5.5	12 £175
3 2	8 7.5 h	13 23p
4 $\frac{3}{13}$	9 56	14 8p
5 102 km/h	10 15	15 10 h

Test 24

1 How far will a car travel at seventy miles per hour if it travels from nine thirty in the morning until noon?

2 What is the area of carpet needed for a rectangular room four metres by three metres which contains a fireplace one and a half metres by one metre?

3 Fifty pounds is divided between two brothers in the ratio of seven to three. How much does each get?

4 What is the probability of obtaining a three when a fair die is rolled?

5 Work out twenty-five per cent of four hundred and sixty pounds.

6 What is the size of the interior angle of a regular quadrilateral?

7 One-half of a group of children are over twelve and a third of the rest are boys. What fraction of the group is boys under twelve?

You will now need your Information Sheet

8 What is the saving when buying a hammer?

9 What is the cost of five, six foot square panels?

10 What is the percentage rise in productivity from ninety eighty-two till nineteen eighty-four stroke eighty-five?

11 What is the difference between half the adult price of a stand seat at the cheapest rate and a juvenile stand seat at the cheapest rate?

12 How much extra is paid back after borrowing one thousand pounds and then repaying the full amount at nineteen pounds ninety-six pence per month?

13 Write the time of the afternoon high tide on Sunday using the twenty-four-hour-clock system.

14 What is the price of five pounds of smoked cod and one pound of cockles?

15 What increase does Vanguard give in one year for every one thousand pounds invested?

ANSWERS

1 175 miles	6 90°	11 £15.50
2 10.5 m^2	7 $\frac{1}{6}$	12 £796.40
3 £35 and £15	8 £1.16	13 13 59
4 $\frac{1}{6}$	9 £42.50	14 £8.10
5 £115	10 6%	15 £269

Test 25

1 What is the approximate cost of four shirts at five pounds ninety-two pence each?

2 What is the next square number after sixty-four?

3 A bag contains four white balls and six red balls. What is the probability of getting a red ball with one dip into the bag?

4 I am twelve minutes early for the five past eight bus. What time did I arrive at the bus stop?

5 In this question *b* has the value three and *c* has the value five. What is the value of six *b* minus four *c*?

6 Write down the size of one of the equal angles in a right-angled isosceles triangle.

7 How much simple interest is earned when one hundred and fifty pounds is invested for three years at five per cent?

You will now need your Information Sheet

8 Five thousand pounds is invested in a Number One Income Account. How much interest has been earned, net, at the end of the first year?

9 What percentage is not classified as general or physical activities under Processes?

10 How much would you expect to pay this firm for a three piece suite normally costing six hundred and eighty-nine pounds?

11 I wish to carpet a room five yards wide and seven yards long for the minimum outlay, not using roll ends. What will it cost?

12 I intend to fence three sides of a garden which is seventy-two feet square, using Lap Fencing. What will it cost?

13 How much is saved on an Astra one point three clutch while it is on offer?

14 Work out **A** plus **B**.

15 How many elements are there in set P?

ANSWERS		
1 £24	6 45°	11 £104.65
2 81	7 £22.50	12 £306
3 $\frac{3}{5}$	8 £400	13 £7.80
4 7:53	9 1%	14 $\left(\begin{smallmatrix} 0 & 5 \\ 2 & 2 \end{smallmatrix}\right)$
5 −2	10 £344.50	15 6

Extension 1

1 What is the sum of nine and twenty-four point two seven?

2 Mr Green makes bolts for which he is paid four pence each. He can produce two hundred bolts in an hour and works for seven and a half hours a day. How much does he earn a day?

3 Vanessa scored seven out of twenty in a test. What percentage is this?

4 The twenty-six letters of the alphabet are placed in a bag. What is the probability that the first letter taken from the bag is a vowel?

5 Two angles in a triangle add up to eighty degrees. What is the size of the third angle?

6 How many square millimetres are equal to a square centimetre?

7 In a school the ratio of staff to pupils is one to eighteen. The school has one hundred and eight pupils. How many staff are there?

You will now need your Information Sheet

8 How long does it take the bus to get from the bus station to the church at Highbridge?

9 How much would ten square yards of carpet cost?

10 The account manager earns fifteen thousand, two hundred pounds. How much commission is this?

11 What is the size of angle *a*?

12 How wide are the doors in inches?

13 What are the co-ordinates of the point marked x?

14 How much would fifty feet of the two inch by one inch timber cost?

15 Write this number to the nearest one thousand.

ANSWERS		
1 33.27	6 100	11 50°
2 £60	7 6	12 30 inches
3 35%	8 58 min	13 (0.5, 1)
4 $\frac{5}{26}$	9 £77.50	14 £3.50
5 100°	10 £3400	15 784 000

Extension 2

1 How many different shapes form the net of an octahedron?

2 What are the two values for the square root of two hundred and eighty-nine?

3 A packet of butter is six times smaller in every dimension than the box in which it is stored. How many packets of butter are there in every box?

4 A ship travelling south-west changes direction by sixty degrees towards west. What is its new bearing?

5 Fifteen, one pound coins stacked on top of each other reach a height of fifty millimetres. How much would a stack measuring eight centimetres be worth?

6 Houses are equally spaced on both sides of a street with even numbers on one side and odd on the other. The houses with odd numbers start earlier than the even numbers because a school is on one corner. Therefore, number two is opposite number seven and four opposite nine. Which number house is opposite number twenty-two?

7 How many digits from one to nine have two lines of symmetry?

You will now need your Information Sheet

8 How much would it cost for a husband, wife and four children, aged eleven, seven, four and two to eat in the family restaurant?

9 How many of the smaller slabs will I need to make a patio fifteen feet long and nine feet wide?

10 Assuming you were paid every four weeks, how much would you get in each pay packet before deductions?

11 What would be the final price of the offer quoted on hardwood, if VAT is charged at fifteen per cent?

12 A TV licence costs fifty-eight pounds a year. What will be the total annual cost of renting the set and buying a licence?

13 Exhausts normally carry an eighteen month guarantee. How much a month does this suggest an exhaust is likely to cost you for an Acclaim to the nearest penny?

14 For how many hours a week is this post office open?

15 A hairdresser works Monday, Wednesday, Friday and Saturday for two pounds twenty an hour. How much will she earn?

ANSWERS

1 1	6 27	11 £3247.60
2 ±17 (both needed)	7 2	12 £193.20
	8 £22.40	13 £3.20
3 216	9 60	14 74h 30min
4 285°	10 £183	15 £80.30
5 £24		

Extension 3

1 There are nine point five francs for each British pound. What would the equivalent price be in francs for something which costs eight pounds in the UK?

2 Give the y-co-ordinate of the point on the line y equals x plus five for which x equals minus one.

3 The first two directions for a yacht to follow a square course are north-east, ten kilometres and south-east, ten kilometres. What is the next instruction?

4 Taking the value of pi as three, work out the area of a circle of radius five centimetres.

5 I invest two hundred pounds at ten per cent interest for two years. I leave the interest to be added to my money at the end of the first year. How much do I have at the end of two years?

6 Add the column matrix one two to the column matrix two three.

7 In a class of thirty-six children aged twelve it is found that the same number of children were born in each of the twelve months of the year. What is the probability of a child being born in November or December?

You will now need your Information Sheet

8 What is the change from a fifty pound note after buying a four zero zero H eighteen T/T tyre?

9 What was the trading loss in nineteen eighty-five stroke eighty-six?

10 How much money was spent on bowls?

11 The cost of loft insulation is two hundred pounds. How much would an OAP with no existing loft insulation pay if receiving rate rebate?

12 Add together the percentage of authorities using Tandy and Acorn computers and give the answer correct to the nearest whole number.

13 Write in figures the number of tonnes of freight expected to be carried in nineteen ninety-three.

14 How much change would I get from twenty pounds when I buy 'British Hit Singles'?

15 What is the total cost of six, style A six hundred and thirty by one thousand, five hundred and twenty millimetre windows?

ANSWERS

1 76FF	6 $\binom{3}{5}$	11 £20
2 4	7 $\frac{1}{6}$	12 81%
3 South-west 10km	8 £15.26	13 84 000 000
4 75cm^2	9 £140 million	14 £12.05
5 £242	10 £195 000	15 £498

Extension 4

1 What is two squared added to three cubed?

2 On August the fifteenth the temperature was eighteen degrees centigrade. On January the twenty-third it was twenty-four degrees colder. What was the temperature on that day?

3 What is the sum of nought point two and a quarter as a decimal?

4 What is the surface area of a cube of side two centimetres?

5 The letters of the word 'factorise' are placed on separate pieces of paper in a bag. One letter is withdrawn. What is the probability of getting a vowel?

6 A paper boy is paid five pence for every ten papers he delivers each day of the week. How much is he paid for delivering sixty papers per day for six days of the week?

7 The exchange rate is nine point five francs for each pound. How many francs would I get for three pounds fifty pence?

You will now need your Information Sheet

8 What is the difference between the most and the least expensive cars advertised?

9 What is the range of numbers appearing in today's game?

10 What was the average (mean) number of Venture Scouts for the three years?

11 I arrived on Thursday afternoon at Old Church at ten past two. How long did I have to wait for the bus to Weston-super-Mare?

12 What is the difference in price between a quality mild-steel exhaust and a long life exhaust for a Carlton?

13 Write in figures the index reading in June nineteen eighty-six.

14 What fraction of the diagram is shaded?

15 What is the total cost of the charts for the Thames Estuary and the Channel Islands?

ANSWERS

1 31	6 £1.80	11 12 min
2 −6°C	7 33.25 F	12 £3.20
3 0.45	8 £22 100	13 1540–1560
4 24 cm²	9 97	14 $\frac{7}{20}$
5 $\frac{4}{9}$	10 72	15 £12.25

Extension 5

1 Two point six Swiss francs can be exchanged for one pound sterling. How many francs will five pounds fifty pence be worth?

2 A man walked two hundred metres in ninety seconds. How long will it take him to walk one kilometre?

3 Posts are placed two metres apart. How many posts will I need to mark off a line twenty-six metres long?

4 The mean of five numbers is four point two. What do all five numbers add up to?

5 Given that x equals three and y equals eight, what is the value of five xy?

6 I invested two hundred pounds in a bank for three years. The interest rate was ten per cent, how much interest did I receive at the end of the first year?

7 Draw a network which has five arcs, three nodes and four regions.

You will now need your Information Sheet

8 How much do I save by planing my own wood if I buy twenty feet of the smallest size Scandinavian Pine and do not pay VAT?

9 How long is the boat being used each day on the route between Oxford and Abingdon?

10 What is the saving on the Vi Spring divans?

11 How much would the first ten lessons cost?

12 How much a month does a secretary earn?

13 I leave home at four thirty in the morning and travel to work which takes one and a half hours. For how long should I have my lights on?

14 What is the difference in price between the two most expensive single-glazed conservatories?

15 VAT is charged at fifteen per cent. What would be the cost of the reduced suite?

ANSWERS

1 14.3 FF	6 £20	11 £66.50
2 7.5 min	7 e.g.	12 £450
3 14		13 28 min
4 21	8 £1	14 £721
5 120	9 7 h 35 min	15 £228.85
	10 £582.50	

Test 1

1 What would be the cost of seven cakes at ninety-eight pence each?

2 What would be the area of a square whose perimeter is thirty-two centimetres?

3 The sun is ninety-three million miles from the earth. Write this number using figures.

4 A car takes four and a half hours to travel three hundred and sixty kilometres. What is its average speed?

5 If a man sets his video to start at seventeen fifty-four and stop at nineteen twenty-seven how long will he be recording for?

6 If a plank, six metres long, is cut into lengths of thirty-five centimetres, how much is left over at the end?

7 A medicine bottle has a capacity of a quarter of a litre. If you need ten millilitres of medicine a day, how long will this bottle last?

You will now need your Information Sheet

8 Estimate the size of the angle shown.

9 If the shop opens at nine a.m. every day, how many hours a week is it open for?

10 At the normal price how many grams of cereals would you expect for one penny?

11 At what time will I arrive at Lower Edmonton if I get to Cambridge Heath at fourteen fifty?

12 How much do you pay a year if you borrow the maximum amount?

13 What fraction of the one point four Ghia old price is the nine hundred and fifty Pop old price?

14 How much will it cost to borrow four thousand pounds over thirty-six months? Give your answer to the nearest one hundred pounds.

15 How much would it cost to sell a house worth forty-five thousand pounds?

ANSWERS

1 £6.86	6 5cm	11 1513
2 64cm²	7 25 days	12 £1632.24
3 93 000 000	8 20°–40°	13 ⅔
4 80km/h	9 65h	14 £5100 or
5 2h33min	10 3–4g	£5200
		15 £225

Test 2

1 What is the difference in temperature between eight hundred and fifty-six degrees Celsius and two hundred and seventy-nine degrees Celsius?

2 Three men worked on repairing a roof. They were paid three pounds sixty pence each an hour. The total wages they received came to fifty-four pounds. How long did they take to do the job?

3 Elaine goes hiking in the country. She walks at an average speed of six kilometres an hour for eight and a half hours during which time she has two hours rest. How many kilometres does she cover?

4 Seventeen school children each eat sixteen sweets. How many sweets do they eat altogether?

5 Pierre had a week's fishing holiday near Paris. The number of fish he caught each day were as follows: nine, twelve, sixteen, none, twenty-three, four and thirteen. What was his average catch per day?

6 Out of a possible four hundred and fifty marks Sonya scored two hundred and seventy. Express her marks as a percentage.

7 There are fourteen pounds in a stone. A boxer weighs in at one hundred and ninety-three pounds. How much is this in stones and pounds?

You will now need your Information Sheet

8 I pay the deposit plus five instalments. How much have I paid so far?

9 The temperature in degrees Celsius in Belgrade is twenty-four degrees. What fraction is this of the temperature in degrees fahrenheit in Geneva?

10 To the nearest pound what is the cost per day of the coach holiday?

11 Andy buys twelve litres of cola for a party. He shares the cost with his two brothers. How much does each pay?

12 Write in words the turnover in pounds for nineteen eighty-seven.

13 Half the countries in which BP employees work employ fifty thousand people. What is the average number of employees in each of the other countries?

14 Each brother is responsible for fifty per cent of the total acreage they own in Imperial Valley. How many acres is each in charge of?

15 Hannah pays for the Rover in eight equal instalments. How much does she pay each time?

ANSWERS

1 577°C	6 60%	11 £1.30
2 5h	7 13 stone 11 lb	12 Two thousand four
3 51km	8 £490.75	hundred and seven
4 272	9 ⅓	million pounds
5 11	10 £18	13 2000
		14 7850 acres
		15 £899.50

Test 3

1 What is the highest common factor of three x squared, twelve x and fifteen x cubed?

2 The sum of all the angles of a regular polygon is three hundred and sixty degrees. Name the polygon.

3 What is the decimal value of two to the power of minus two?

4 A journey represented by the column vector two, one follows one represented by the vector three, minus two. What vector represents the combined journey?

5 How many minutes are there between nine nineteen and fifteen thirty-two?

6 A number written in standard form correct to two significant figures is six point six times ten to the four. Write in decimal form the smallest value this number could be.

7 Taking pi as three, work out the area of a circle whose circumference is forty-two centimetres.

You will now need your Information Sheet

8 What is the cost of two adults, in the best seats, and one child for a performance on the twelfth of January?

9 What is the mean (average) number of hours per day that the pitch is open to the public? Give your answer as a fraction.

10 What was the approximate range of values for platinum in July?

11 What is the cost of a nest of tables and a video cabinet?

12 Estimate the angle of the sector for insurance in nineteen eighty-six.

13 Approximately how many scientists were employed doing pure research during nineteen eighty-two?

14 It is estimated that operating profits will increase by twenty per cent next year. What will they be?

15 What would be the cost of three, nine carat gold, sixteen inch Figaro chains?

ANSWERS

1 3x	6 65 500	11 £218
2 Square	7 147 cm²	12 160°–170°
3 0.25	8 £11.05	13 130 000–
4 $\binom{5}{-1}$	9 $2\frac{5}{14}$ h	140 000
5 373 min	10 550–590	14 1380 m
		15 £52.47

Test 4

1 What is the average of ninety-seven, sixty-three, eighty-five and eighty-one?

2 Mike was paid four pounds fifty pence for his weekly paper round. His employer gave him a thirty per cent rise. How much was he then earning?

3 A food mixer revolves at three times a second. How many revolutions does it make in a minute and a half?

4 How many must be added to eight hundred and sixty-four to make twelve thousand and six?

5 Angle a of a triangle measures twenty-seven degrees and angle b is twice as wide as angle a. What does angle c measure?

6 Postman Pat delivered mail to one hundred and eighty houses. At Christmas his tips averaged twenty-six pence from each house. How much did he collect altogether?

7 There are three feet in a yard. A small playing area is thirty-six feet long and seven yards wide. What is its area in square yards?

You will now need your Information Sheet

8 A merchant buys five gold diamond rings and is allowed a ten per cent discount. To the nearest fifty pence how much does he pay?

9 Jane Betteridge ran four minutes forty seconds slower than her best-ever time for a marathon. What time did she record?

10 Excluding commission what is the total annual wage bill for two warehouse assistants and one sales assistant?

11 Debenhams have recently increased the price of king-sized quilts by one twentieth. How much did one cost before the increase?

12 What is the floor area of a cage for white leghorns?

13 Wayne needed seventy-five German marks for a brief visit to Berlin. How many pounds (rounded up to the nearest pound) need he change to get this number of marks?

14 Seven chickadees laid fifty-one eggs between them. Five of them each lay the maximum number of eggs. How many does each of the others lay?

15 The guided visit to the pirate ship costs two pounds seventy pence for adults, half price for children. Mr and Mrs Williams took their five children on the visit. How much did it cost them?

ANSWERS

1 81.5	6 £46.80	11 £79.99
2 £5.85	7 84 yard²	12 288 inch²
3 270	8 £63	13 £26
4 11 142	9 4 h 16 min 54 s	14 5 and 6
5 99°	10 £18 940	15 £12.15

Test 5

1 What is the average (mean) temperature over four days when the temperatures were five degrees, two degrees, zero degrees and minus three degrees?

2 Point four of a class of thirty children are girls. How many of the class are boys?

3 Estimate the square root of eight thousand, one hundred.

4 Two sides of a right-angled triangle are four centimetres and five centimetres. What is the area of the triangle? All three sides of the triangle are integral values.

5 What is the area of the net for an open rectangular box seven by four by three centimetres? The missing side is seven by four centimetres.

6 Carpet squres are advertised as one metre square to the nearest centimetre. What is the largest and smallest size in millimetres each side could be?

7 A bricklayer is paid a rate of five pounds per hour eight hours per day, time and a half for overtime and a bonus of five pence per brick laid over a certain limit. What does he get paid for a day in which he worked nine hours and laid one hundred bonus bricks?

You will now need your Information Sheet

8 This is part of the bill from a French hypermarket. What is the total cost of the first eight items, in francs?

9 What is the approximate temperature at which the expansion coefficient is a minimum?

10 What is the probability of obtaining a prime number?

11 Discount is taken off before VAT at fifteen per cent is added. What will I pay when I order a kitchen to the value of two thousand, four hundred pounds?

12 I bought a Y registered Suzuki GS one two five by paying twenty-four payments of thirty pounds. How much more than the cash price did I pay?

13 How much does a one nine five stroke seventy HR by fourteen tyre cost including VAT at fifteen per cent?

14 Write the approximate money spent in nineteen eighty-two in figures.

15 What is the diameter of the tunnel in metres? (Use your ruler.)

ANSWERS		
1 1°	6 1005 mm and	11 £2070
2 18	995 mm	12 £125
3 90	7 £52.50	13 £40.25
4 6 cm²	8 34.60 FF	14 £8 400 000 –
5 94 cm²	9 23 – 27 K	£8 800 000
	10 $\frac{1}{6}$	15 5.7 – 6.7 m

Test 6

1 In a football match the ball goes out of play once every three minutes. When the ball goes out of play for the twenty-fourth time how long has the match been in progress?

2 The sea comes in twice a day at a seaside resort. How many times will the sea come in during the month of July?

3 The area of a field is six hundred square yards. The field is thirty yards long. How wide is it?

4 I buy bags of crisps for a party. How much money will I need to buy seventeen bags if they cost eleven pence each?

5 Two trains are approaching each other from opposite directions. They start three hundred and eighty-five miles apart. If one is travelling at fifty miles an hour and the other at sixty miles an hour how long will it be before they meet?

6 Two people build a boat in six weeks. How many boats could four people build in twelve weeks?

7 A car is bought for three thousand pounds. It is then sold at a profit of nine per cent. What is the selling price?

You will now need your Information Sheet

8 A man bought a whole New Zealand lamb for thirty-nine pounds. How heavy was it?

9 A girl went on holiday and used an Aussiepass to get around. She travelled an average of forty miles a day. How much does this cost her per mile to the nearest penny?

10 What is the difference in degrees Celsius between the hottest sunny day and the coldest fair day?

11 How much would one volume cost, to the nearest penny?

12 A school needs another three people to go on a visit in order to get its fifth free place. How many people have said they wish to go so far?

13 Approximately how far is it across the volcanic crater lake from one side to the other, passing through the centre?

14 The line shown forms part of a map using a scale of one to twenty-five thousand, estimate the distance this represents, in real terms. Give your answer in kilometres.

15 What was the percentage rise in prices between nineteen eighty-four and nineteen eighty-five?

ANSWERS		
1 72 min	6 4	11 £4
2 62	7 £3270	12 37
3 20 yards	8 50 lb	13 1.4 – 1.7 km
4 £1.87	9 25p	14 20 – 25 km
5 3.5 h	10 6 °C	15 25%

Test 7

1 The mean of five numbers is six point two. What is their sum?

2 How much simple interest is earned when three hundred and fifty pounds is invested for two years at an interest rate of eight per cent per annum?

3 What is the sum of the fourth row of Pascal's triangle?

4 Ninety people took part in a political survey. Twenty-six of them said they voted Conservative. What size angle represents this group of people on a pie chart?

5 A kitchen unit has a length of six hundred millimetres. How many units can be placed in a space two point five metres wide?

6 Which of these shapes is not a quadrilateral: rhombus, rectangle, hexagon, kite or trapezium?

7 What is the reciprocal of one-quarter?

You will now need your Information Sheet

8 How much, in kilograms, would twenty of these packs of yogurt weigh?

9 Estimate the three figure bearing of Lumbfoot from Keighley.

10 What is the sum of the nodes and regions for this network?

11 How much would five hundred units have cost in eighty-five stroke six?

12 What would be the monthly income on an investment of twelve thousand pounds?

13 This is part of a regular polygon. What type of polygon is it?

14 Which of these letters have rotational symmetry of order two?

15 What was the mean temperature in degrees Celsius of the first three towns?

ANSWERS		
1 31	6 Hexagon	11 £10.38
2 £56	7 4	12 £105
3 8	8 30 kg	13 Pentagon
4 104°	9 230°–245°	14 O and N
5 4	10 6	15 27°C

Test 8

1 Write the number twenty-seven point zero three two nine correct to one decimal place.

2 The average (mean) of three numbers is seven. If two of the numbers are six and twelve what is the third?

3 Write one-eighth as a decimal fraction.

4 I buy pens for fifty pence and sell them for sixty-five pence. What percentage profit is that?

5 Where does the line y equals two x plus one cross the y-axis, i.e. the line x equals nought?

6 A bicycle wheel has a radius of thirty centimetres. Taking pi as three, estimate how many times the wheel must revolve to travel one hundred metres.

7 A ship's captain notices a lighthouse on a bearing of nought eight three degrees. On what bearing will the lighthouse keeper observe the ship?

You will now need your Information Sheet

8 Give an approximation in square inches for the area of the second radiator on the list.

9 Give the approximate cost per centilitre of the ginger ale. The prices are in sterling.

10 What is the approximate percentage saving on the purchase of a Philips one zero one four portable colour television?

11 What is the cost of the Saturday, August the first trip to Ilfracombe for two adults and one child?

12 What is the cost of twelve metres of fifteen millimetre copper tube plus VAT at fifteen per cent? Give your answer to the nearest ten pence.

13 Estimate the average inflation rate during nineteen eighty-seven.

14 How much VAT is paid on a set of five, two zero five stroke seventy HR fourteen tyres?

15 What is the total cost of a dishwasher and a washing machine?

ANSWERS		
1 27.0	6 50–60 times	11 £22.40
2 3	7 263°	12 £10.10
3 0.125	8 600 inch²	13 3.5–4.5%
4 30%	9 3p	14 £33.75
5 $y = 1$	10 11%	15 £369.90

Test 9

1 What is the product of forty and fifty?

2 In a test Aaron scored eleven out of twenty. What percentage is this?

3 When two dice are rolled what is the probability of getting a double one?

4 How many twenty-four millimetre pieces of metal can be cut from a two metre length of metal?

5 A triangle has sides of six, eight and ten centimetres. What type of triangle is this?

6 Frances buys three bars of soap and receives nineteen pence change from one pound. How many bars of soap could she buy with five pounds?

7 How many lines of symmetry has a kite?

You will now need your Information Sheet

8 What would be the total cost for a party of thirty people attending on Friday the tenth in the evening?

9 Which letters have rotational symmetry order two?

10 Estimate the three figure bearing of Brighton from Maidstone.

11 What is the total price of this van from the garage?

12 Write the nineteen eighty-seven group turnover in figures.

13 The scale of this map is one centimetre to one kilometre. Estimate the actual length of railway line shown.

14 The estate agents receive a two per cent commission. How much would they earn for selling this house at the advertised price?

15 A bed in this sale costs sixty pounds. How much has been saved?

ANSWERS

1 2000	6 18	11 £3680
2 55%	7 1	12 £4 220 800 000
3 $\frac{1}{36}$	8 £165	13 6–8 km
4 83	9 I and S	14 £1900
5 Right-angled	10 215°–245°	15 £20

Test 10

1 A motorist travels sixteen miles in twelve minutes. What is his average speed in miles per hour?

2 In a class of thirty-five children three-sevenths are boys. How many girls are there in the class?

3 Peter bought seven copies of a book. He gave the shopkeeper thirty pounds and received four pounds fifty-nine pence change. How much was each book?

4 The bearing of Newtown from Highgate is one four six degrees. What is the bearing of Highgate from Newtown?

5 The sun rises at six a.m. and sets at ten p.m. What percentage of the day is in daylight?

6 Concrete is made from gravel, sand and cement in the ratio of three to two to one, respectively. How much sand is used to make one point two tonnes of concrete?

7 How many lines of symmetry does a scalene triangle have?

You will now need your Information Sheet

8 How much would three pounds of corned beef cost?

9 What was the mean height of the two tides on Thursday?

10 Express sine theta as a fully simplified fraction.

11 How much are the yearly repayments on a one thousand pound loan over ten years?

12 How many patio paving slabs are required to cover a rectangular area measuring thirty feet by nine feet?

13 The lines XY and YZ are two sides of a regular polygon. How many sides does this polygon have?

14 How much does an A-five leaflet cost?

15 Estimate the three figure bearing of A from B.

ANSWERS

1 80 m.p.h.	6 0.4 tonnes	11 £211.64
2 20	7 None	12 120
3 £3.63	8 £3.16	13 12
4 326°	9 10.6 m	14 0.85p
5 66$\frac{2}{3}$%	10 $\frac{4}{5}$	15 265°–280°

LEVEL 2

Test 11

1 A shopkeeper buys cassette tapes at fourteen pounds for twenty and sells them for one pound and five pence each. What percentage profit does he make?

2 John divides his bar of chocolate and eats half today. Tomorrow he will eat a quarter of what he has left. What fraction of the whole bar will he have left after eating tomorrow's piece?

3 A motor cycle advertised for one thousand, five hundred and fifty pounds can be bought for ten per cent deposit and twenty-four monthly payments of eighty-five pounds. What is the total cost of the monthly payments?

4 Write the number seventy point three six five correct to three significant figures.

5 A piece of wire thirty-six centimetres long is bent, and cut where necessary, to form the edges of a cube. How long is each edge?

6 Write down the prime factors of twenty-four.

7 A dustbin with a diameter of fifteen inches is said to contain twenty-five litres. How much would a similar shaped dustbin contain with a diameter of thirty inches?

You will now need your Information Sheet

8 What is the mean (average) temperature in centigrade of the British towns beginning with the letter B?

9 What is the cost of three, twelve inch, spicy vegetarian pizzas with extra garlic on each?

10 Approximately how many non-railway staff were employed in nineteen eighty-three?

11 What is the total amount paid back after borrowing two thousand pounds and paying it back in three years?

12 In response to the Eurotunnel the aircraft improves its time by ten per cent. How long does it now take?

13 Estimate the size of the sector representing Africa in nineteen eighty-four.

14 What was the total number of minutes spent on motor racing?

15 What is the cost of a short advert, including VAT, which takes two lines?

ANSWERS

1 50%	6 2 and 3	11 £2580.24
2 $\frac{3}{8}$	7 100 litres	12 2 h 42 min
3 £2040	8 22°C	13 35°–45°
4 70.4	9 £11.65	14 2492 min
5 3 cm	10 42 000–48 000	15 £21.85

Test 12

1 How many litres of water are required to fill a rectangular bowl measuring fifty centimetres by twenty centimetres by ten centimetres?

2 What is the sum of negative twenty, fourteen and negative nine?

3 A box of twenty-four bars of chocolate cost two pounds sixty-five pence. When all the bars are sold, a profit of two pounds fifteen pence is made. What is the selling price of a bar of chocolate?

4 What is the surface area of a cube with edges of one point five centimetres?

5 In a class of thirty-six children twenty are boys. When selecting a child from the class, what is the probability of choosing a girl?

6 How long would it take a motorist to travel forty-five kilometres when averaging sixty kilometres an hour?

7 A company offers to process a twenty-four print film for one pound eighty pence. How much per print is this?

You will now need your Information Sheet

8 Using these packs, how much would it cost to give thirty-five people two bags of crisps each?

9 Write the eighty-six stroke seven sales of units in figures.

10 How much would it cost to rent a Sierra for one year, excluding VAT?

11 How many US dollars would you get for fifty pounds?

12 Estimate the area of this rectangle in square centimetres.

13 What is the approximate percentage saving per pound of lamb?

14 Estimate the three figure bearing of Bristol from Malmesbury.

15 What is the size of the angle marked b?

ANSWERS

1 10	6 45 min	11 80
2 −15	7 7.5p	12 9–13 cm²
3 20p	8 £5.90	13 13–14%
4 13.5 cm²	9 232 900 000 000 units	14 210°–250°
5 $\frac{4}{9}$	10 £2235.48	15 100°

LEVEL 2

Test 13

1 A woman buys a car for one thousand pounds and sells it later for nine hundred pounds. What was her percentage loss?

2 A bus leves Wimbledon at eleven forty-three and arrives in Putney at twelve thirteen. Putney is four point five miles from Wimbledon. Calculate the average speed of the bus.

3 A biased coin has a probability of nought point four of landing heads. What is the probability of it landing tails?

4 What is the square of one-third?

5 What are the dimensions of the rectangle with the greatest area that can be made from a piece of wire forty-four centimetres long?

6 Geoffrey buys five packs of three pens and receives three pounds ninety-five pence change from five pounds. What is the cost of a single pen?

7 What is the size of one exterior angle of a regular pentagon?

You will now need your Information Sheet

8 What is the percentage saving on the Charnwood suite?

9 Write this figure in standard form.

10 Estimate the three figure bearing of Southampton from Brighton.

11 Give the co-ordinates of A after a reflection in the y-axis.

12 Which of these letters have one line of symmetry?

13 How long is there between high tides on Thursday?

14 How much will a stereo normally priced at eighty-six pounds cost in this sale?

15 Calculate the size of angle b?

ANSWERS

1 10%	6 7p	11 (3, −1)
2 9 m.p.h.	7 72°	12 E and W
3 0.6	8 20%	13 12 h 23 min
4 $\frac{1}{9}$	9 8.74248 × 10⁵	14 £68.80
5 11 cm × 11 cm	10 275°–290°	15 70°

Test 14

1 There are one hundred and twelve furlongs in fourteen miles. How many furlongs are there in a mile?

2 Write in figures the number one million, seven thousand and eight.

3 l equals seven and p equals one. What is the value of p to the power of nine multiplied by l squared?

4 Add nine and two-fifths to forty-eight and three-quarters.

5 In an election twenty-one thousand people voted. For every four people who voted for Smith, three people voted for Brown. How many voted for Brown?

6 Write this number to three places of decimals: one hundred and six point zero four six seven.

7 How many days are there in any four successive years?

You will now need your Information Sheet

8 Estimate how many tourists came from Japan in nineteen eighty-two.

9 Given that two million people work in Hong Kong, how many are employed in manufacturing?

10 Approximately how many people were eligible to vote in all the eleven boroughs shown as 'about five hundred' on the diagram?

11 This offer does not include VAT at fifteen per cent. I need BMW twins with a round filter and an oil cooler. What will be the total bill?

12 The owner eventually sells this machine for ten per cent less than the advertisement states. What was the final sale price to the nearest pound?

13 How many of these people are not employed along the Fraser?

14 At this time there were an equal number of women and men in Tibet. How many people lived there in nineteen fifty-nine?

15 Prices since nineteen eighty-four have risen by ten per cent. What would be the present price of the goggles?

ANSWERS

1 8	6 106.047	11 £27.60
2 1 007 008	7 1461	12 £2700
3 49	8 1 600 000–	13 76 500
4 58$\frac{3}{20}$	1 740 000	14 960 000
5 9000	9 740 000	15 £18.97 or
	10 5500	£18.98

Test 15

1 Antifreeze, which is sold in one, two and a half, or five litre containers, must be mixed to form a twenty-five per cent mixture with the cooling system water. Which quantity should I buy for my car which has an eighteen litre cooling system?

2 Mrs Sengh measures the height of her window to fit curtains. It was thirty-seven inches and needed two lengths of material. What length of material should she buy to be sure of having enough, but not to waste too much? Answer in feet and inches.

3 A long playing record revolves thirty-three and a third times every minute. In one song I counted that it revolved approximately two hundred and thirty-three times. How long was the song?

4 What is the nearest whole number to the square root of one hundred and ninety?

5 A calculator display shows six point seven three two then a space then nine. What number does the display represent?

6 Last night the temperature fell to minus six point five degrees. That was one point two degrees warmer than the previous night. What was the temperature then?

7 What is the interior angle of a regular hexagon?

You will now need your Information Sheet

8 What is the cost of each computer label?

9 What is the approximate percentage saving when buying a JVC C one forty EK fourteen inch TV?

10 I wish to arrive at Cheddar by five p.m. What time should I catch a bus at Marine Parade, Weston-super-Mare?

11 Approximately how many yen could be purchased for a dollar during February?

12 In which occupations might one be better off if employed by a UK-owned company?

13 The exchange rate is nine francs fifty to the pound. What is the approximate cost in sterling of a litre of fresh milk, i.e. lait frais?

14 What is the approximate percentage saving when using gas after having the loft and walls insulated?

15 How much interest would be earned when investing fifteen thousand pounds for one year?

ANSWERS

1 5 litres	6 −7.7°	11 152−154 yen
2 6 feet 6 inches−	7 120°	12 Industrial
7 feet 6 inches	8 0.5875p	equipment
3 7 min	9 10%	manufacturing,
4 14	10 16 15	financial
5 6 732 000 000		services,
		consumer
		services and
		construction
		13 44−46p
		14 37−43%
		15 £1162.50

Test 16

1 A journey of twenty-four miles took twenty minutes. What was the average speed for this journey?

2 Exercise books come in packs of twenty-five. How many packs are required to give each pupil in a class of thirty, eight books each?

3 A kitchen floor measures four point six metres by two point eight metres. How many square floor tiles with edges of twenty centimetres are required to cover the floor?

4 What is the cube root of sixty-four?

5 The bearing of High Wycombe from Beaconsfield is two hundred degrees. What is the bearing of Beaconsfield from High Wycombe?

6 Ed Moses improved on his world record time of forty-seven point nought eight seconds by fifteen-hundredths of a second. What was his new record time?

7 One method of changing degrees centigrade into degrees Fahrenheit is to multiply by one point eight and then add thirty-two. Change ten degrees centigrade to degrees Fahrenheit.

You will now need your Information Sheet

8 A room costs one hundred and seventy-five pounds to carpet using the most expensive carpet. What is the area of the room?

9 What percentage saving will the sixth customer of the day receive?

10 What is the difference between the last two years' efficiency figures?

11 The test fee is fifteen per cent of the course fee. How much is this test fee?

12 To the nearest month, what is the difference in the ages of the fighters?

13 How much would a forty-eight year old person choosing Plan A have to pay each year?

14 What is the approximate percentage saving?

15 Express angle y in terms of x.

ANSWERS

1 72 m.p.h.	6 46.93 s	11 £39.75
2 10	7 50°F	12 7 years
3 322	8 14 yard^2	6 months
4 4	9 70%	13 £111.60
5 020°	10 0.43%	14 13−16%
		15 4.5x

Test 17

1 An ice-hockey match consists of sixty minutes actual playing time, but players do not play for the whole match. Stefan was on the ice for seven-twelfths of the match. For how many minutes did he play?

2 A weekend break holiday cost one hundred and thirty-nine pounds fifty pence. The cost was shared between Wayne, Les and Alan. How much did each pay?

3 Convert one-quarter of seventy-one to a decimal number.

4 w equals seven, x equals nine and y equals five. What is y squared plus w times x?

5 A cross-country Canadian train leaves Toronto at seven forty-eight on Monday evening. It arrives at its destination at a quarter past five on Wednesday morning. How many hours and minutes did the journey take?

6 Eighty people went on a trip to the seaside. Twenty-five went on the pier. One-fifth of the rest went to look round the shops. How many were left?

7 A used-car salesman sells twelve cars on the first day. On succeeding days he sells nine cars, fifteen cars and eighteen cars. How many must he sell on the next day to average thirteen per day?

You will now need your Information Sheet

8 How much more would the credit price be if the terms quoted are for two years?

9 What was the modal number of goals scored by these teams? The figures in heavy black type are the number of goals scored so far this season by each team.

10 What is the ratio of Siyi to Chaozhou people in Hong Kong in simplified terms?

11 Estimate the distance from Miami to Great Exuma.

12 Approximately how much of Hong Kong's invisible trade in nineteen seventy-eight came from tourism?

13 Children's prices are sixty per cent of the prices quoted. How much would a child's holiday in the Algarve cost?

14 Calculate the size of the angle marked b.

15 What was the approximate index value of food production in nineteen fifty-five?

ANSWERS

1	35 min	6	44	11	350–500 km
2	£46.50	7	11	12	$3000–$4000
3	17.75	8	£14.05	13	£166.80
4	88	9	1	14	105°
5	33 h 27 min	10	3:2	15	104–106

Test 18

1 The perimeter of a rectangle is increased by a factor of three, keeping the proportions of the rectangle the same. By how much is the area increased?

2 What decimal fraction is equivalent to one-eighth?

3 When multiplying three point six by twenty-two point seven five the string of numbers eight five nine zero is obtained. Put the decimal point in the correct place.

4 The heights of Mary and Bushra are one point one metres and one point three two metres. Both heights are correct to the nearest centimetre. What is the biggest possible difference between their heights?

5 What is twenty-five to the power of one-half?

6 Write down the smallest number which is a multiple of three, five and twelve.

7 A man walks three kilometres north and four kilometres east. How far is he directly from his starting point?

You will now need your Information Sheet

8 In nineteen eighty-three how many more years of manganese production were predicted than was thought likely in nineteen seventy-two?

9 How much remains to be paid after paying a ten per cent deposit on the two forty estate?

10 Estimate the distance from Peshawar to Gilgit.

11 What was the median number of recommendations?

12 What would be the cost of three, one eight five stroke sixty HR times fourteen tyres?

13 What is the cost of an antique pine bed and a double divan?

14 On what amount of money is interest charged when taking out this credit facility?

15 What is the cost of one black plastic refuse sack if bought in a lot of four hundred (correct to the nearest penny)?

ANSWERS

1	9	6	60	11	3.5
2	0.125	7	5 km	12	£106.80
3	85.90	8	120 years	13	£209.98
4	23 cm	9	£5125.50	14	£2694.05
5	±5	10	180–220 miles	15	5p

Test 19

1 Write the fifth row of Pascal's triangle.

2 How far will a missile travel in one minute when travelling at one hundred and fifty metres per second? Give your answer in kilometres.

3 What is the cube root of eight squared?

4 Give the new co-ordinates of the point negative two, three after reflection in the x-axis.

5 How much interest is received when five hundred pounds is invested for three years at six per cent simple interest?

6 What is the surface area of a cube with a volume of one hundred and twenty-five cubic centimetres?

7 How many edges does a square-based pyramid have?

You will now need your Information Sheet

8 One-fifth of the enquiries about the share offer come from London. How many enquiries come from there in three days?

9 How many inches longer is the perimeter of one of the front mats than that of one of the back mats?

10 Each bun sells for seventeen pence. How much would you receive if you sold all the buns from two tins?

11 You added two thousand pounds to your minimum investment every six months for three years. Not including interest, how much would you then have invested?

12 To the nearest penny, how much would each polyanthus cost if I bought fifty?

13 Children can go on holiday to Vienna for sixty pounds less than adults. What would it cost Mr and Mrs Jenkins and their two children to go on this four day break?

14 Pauline pays her travel agent the price of her holiday to North India in six equal instalments. How much does she pay each time?

15 Each football match lasted for an hour and a half. QPR scored only four times during the five matches. On average to the nearest ten minutes, how often do they score?

ANSWERS

1 14641	6 150 cm²	11 £22 000
2 9 km	7 8	12 33p
3 4	8 90 000	13 £992
4 (−2, −3)	9 25 inches	14 £77.50
5 £90	10 £4.08	15 110 min

Test 20

1 Jill buys three rolls at fifteen pence each and a cup of coffee. She receives thirty pence change from a one pound coin. How much did the coffee cost?

2 A bar of chocolate is cut into quarters and each quarter is halved. What decimal fraction of the bar is each of the smaller pieces?

3 Between which two whole numbers does the square root of one hundred and seventy-five lie?

4 A cuboid is seven centimetres long, five centimetres wide and three centimetres high. What is the combined area of the two ends?

5 I get twelve and a half per cent discount if I buy a television for cash. How much will I pay for a set normally priced at two hundred and fifty pounds?

6 How long will it take an aeroplane averaging six hundred miles an hour to cover a distance of two thousand, one hundred miles?

7 Solve the equation three x minus four equals minus thirteen.

You will now need your Information Sheet

8 Estimate the nought to sixty miles an hour acceleration time for the nine eleven Turbo.

9 How much will it cost to camp on July the nineteenth and July the twentieth for two adults and a nine year old child?

10 How much longer per week would you work in the sales department at Shepton Mallet Motors than as a mechanic?

11 A family goes to this sale and buys two pairs of swimming trunks, three check shirts, a Berkertex dress and two polycotton tops. How much did they spend?

12 The percentage discount has been blanked out on this advertisement. Use your judgement to find an item which would make it easier to calculate the discount and write the rate to the nearest per cent.

13 The bag of organic fertilizer will cover sixty square metres. What area will one litre cover?

14 Taking account of VAT how much is saved buying a pair of shock absorbers rather than one this week and one next week?

15 I need eight of the six foot by three foot fencing panels and sufficient five foot posts. What will this cost?

ANSWERS

1 25p	6 3.5 h	11 £27.94
2 0.125	7 −3	12 20−25%
3 13 and 14	8 5.5 s	13 1.5 m²
4 30 cm²	9 £11	14 £1.20
5 £218.75	10 6.5 h	15 £72.35

Test 21

1 Write two thirds as a percentage to the nearest whole number.

2 What would be the area of a circle of radius five centimetres, if pi equals three point one?

3 The bearing of A from B is one hundred and ten degrees, what would be the bearing of B from A?

4 What would be the surface area of a cube whose volume is one hundred and twenty-five cubic centimetres?

5 How many lines of symmetry has a regular pentagon?

6 Nine and a half francs are equivalent to one pound sterling. How many pounds are one hundred and ninety-two francs worth?

7 Write down the number which is one smaller than four million.

You will now need your Information Sheet

8 How much will it cost for a family consisting of a husband, wife and three children aged seventeen, eight and four to eat at this restaurant?

9 How much do I save by buying a ten kilogram box rather than the same amount in five hundred gram boxes?

10 Approximately, how many more primary school children are expected in nineteen ninety-one than secondary school children?

11 Which place with fair weather had the hottest temperature?

12 What is the extra saving between the five door rather than the four door, two litre LX diesel Bluebird, using the fleet prices?

13 What would be the cost for a man to insulate a roof if he is given a quotation of two hundred pounds plus VAT at fifteen per cent and receives a local authority grant of twenty-five per cent off the final price?

14 Should this information be displayed on a pie chart, what would be the angle representing the Conservatives in February?

15 What is the approximate percentage saving on the three foot Sleepeezee bed: ten per cent, twenty per cent, thirty per cent or forty per cent?

ANSWERS

1 67%	6 £20.21	11 Corfu
2 77.5 cm²	7 3 999 999	12 £195
3 290°	8 £21.80	13 £172.50
4 150 cm²	9 £2	14 108°
5 5	10 1 million – 1.5 million	15 20%

Test 22

1 What is the square root of six thousand, four hundred?

2 What angle has a tangent value of one?

3 What is the height of a triangle whose area is twenty-four square centimetres and whose base is eight centimetres long?

4 Which of the following shapes will not tessellate on its own: a square, a hexagon, a pentagon or an isosceles triangle?

5 About how many four fluid ounce glasses of wine can be poured from a bottle of wine which holds one pint?

6 How many seconds are there in a ninety minute football match?

7 What is the total length between eleven posts each spaced eight and a half metres apart?

You will now need your Information Sheet

8 What is the cheapest BMC reconditioned engine including fitting?

9 How much will this machine cost in total during April nineteen eighty-seven if VAT is charged at fifteen per cent?

10 What is the difference between the cover for a smoker and a non-smoker if they are both thirty-nine years old and each pay twelve pounds fifty pence per month?

11 How many hours a week is this job for?

12 How long is it between tides on a Friday?

13 How much extra would you pay for the more expensive four foot six inch, rather than the three foot sprung edge divan set in the sale?

14 If the estate agents get two per cent commission for selling the house, how much do they receive?

15 What is the percentage saving roughly: twenty per cent, thirty per cent or fifty per cent?

ANSWERS

1 80	6 5400 s	11 14 h 45 min
2 45°	7 85 m	12 12 h 29 min
3 6 cm	8 £205	13 £104
4 Pentagon	9 £1840	14 £1140
5 5	10 £17 209	15 30%

Test 23

1 A right angled triangle has a hypotenuse of ten centimetres and a base of six centimetres. What is its area?

2 What is the value of six, raised to the power of three?

3 How many lines of symmetry does a regular pentagon have?

4 What is the probability of picking either a red card or a queen from a normal pack of cards?

5 A man's car travels at an average speed of forty-eight kilometres per hour over a distance of seventy-two kilometres. At what time would he expect to finish the journey if he started out at one p.m.?

6 You can exchange a British pound for seventeen Austrian shillings. How many pounds is eighty-five shillings worth?

7 What is the median of the first five triangle numbers?

You will now need your Information Sheet

8 How much extra a week will a bank clerk earn if she is paid two pounds an hour for the additional opening time?

9 How many points do you get for winning a match?

10 How much will I have to pay to cover a ten foot by six foot patio with two foot slabs?

11 Which country has nearly the same unemployment rate as conservation volunteers?

12 What is the total cost of renting the house in Berinsfield for a year?

13 What is the percentage saving being offered on the number two size pellets?

14 A tray holds thirty eggs, how much would you expect to pay for it?

15 How many hours a week is this show room open for?

ANSWERS

1 24 cm²	6 £5	11 Sweden
2 216	7 6	12 £4080
3 5	8 £15	13 25%
4 $\frac{28}{52}$ or $\frac{7}{13}$	9 2	14 £2.40
5 2:30 p.m.	10 £29.25	15 65 h

Test 24

1 A missile travels a distance of one thousand miles in four minutes. At what speed is it travelling in miles per hour?

2 How many carpet tiles half a metre square are needed to carpet a room seven metres by four point seven metres

3 Mortar is to be made with five units of sand to two of cement. How much cement is required to make thirty-five bags of dry mortar?

4 What is the probability of getting two heads when a penny is tossed twice?

5 Estimate the area of a rectangular room twenty-seven point six three feet long by four point two three feet wide. Give your answer to the nearest five square feet.

6 What is the size of the exterior angle of a regular hexagon?

7 Add together one-third of one-half, a half and a third.

You will now need your Information Sheet

8 What is the total cost of a saw and a ladder?

9 What is the cheapest price per foot of the posts? Answer to the nearest penny.

10 What is the average rise in productivity from nineteen eighty-two to nineteen eighty-seven per year?

11 How much is saved at the full rate by buying a family ticket rather than two adults and two juveniles?

12 Ann borrows one thousand pounds for a second-hand car. She repays the loan at twenty-five pounds and seven pence per month. After how many months will she have repaid the original one thousand pounds?

13 What is the average height of the tides on Sunday?

14 What is the price of ten pounds of fresh cod fillet and five pounds of kippers?

15 How much more does Vanguard offer in one year than a building society share account?

ANSWERS

1 15 000 m.p.h.	6 60°	11 £85
2 140	7 1	12 40 months
3 10 bags	8 £46.94	13 9.95 m
4 $\frac{1}{4}$	9 41p	14 £17.10
5 115–120 feet²	10 2.4%	15 £211

Test 25

1 What is the approximate cost of eleven drinks at eighty-eight pence each?

2 What is the next square number after three cubed?

3 A bag contains four white balls and six red balls. A ball is taken from the bag, replaced and another taken. What is the probability that they are both red?

4 I got to my seat in the cinema six minutes before the main film started at five forty. My friend arrived at five forty-four, how long ahead of him was I?

5 In this question b has the value of three and c has the value of minus two. What is the value of c squared minus b squared?

6 The exterior angle of an equilateral triangle is bisected. What size is the angle obtained?

7 One hundred and fifty pounds is invested at six per cent simple interest and earns twenty-seven pounds. For how long was it invested?

You will now need your Information Sheet

8 Five thousand pounds is invested in the Special Three Month Account. How much interest has been earned, net, at the end of the first year?

9 What is the size of the unclassified percentage under Physical Terms?

10 I pay three hundred and forty-eight pounds fifty for a three piece suite. What is the normal price?

11 I wish to carpet a room five yards wide and seven yards long with the most expensive carpet. What will it cost?

12 How many hours per week is this firm open?

13 How much cheaper is a clutch for a rear wheel drive Cavalier than a front wheel drive Cavalier, while on offer?

14 Work out **A** minus **B**.

15 How many elements are there in M and P but not S?

ANSWERS

1 £9.90±30p	6 60°	11 £1154.65
2 36	7 3 years	12 59.5 h
3 $\frac{9}{25}$	8 £412.50	13 £6.85
4 10 min	9 11%	14 $\begin{pmatrix} 2 & -1 \\ -2 & 2 \end{pmatrix}$
5 −5	10 £697	15 11

Extension 1

1 How many equilateral triangles form an icosahedron?

2 What is the value of thirty-two raised to the power minus two-fifths?

3 A two hundred and fifty gram packet of butter is similar in shape to the box in which it is packed but its length is six times smaller. What is the total weight of the butter in a box in kilograms?

4 A ship leaves port sailing south-east. It then changes direction by seventy degrees clockwise. What direction is the ship now facing? Give your answer as a bearing.

5 Fifteen, one pound coins stacked on top of one another reach a height of fifty millimetres. How much would a stack be worth that reached the top of a school hall which was eight metres high?

6 Houses are equally spaced on both sides of a street with even numbers on one side and odd on the other. A school is at the corner on one side so number two is opposite number seven, and four opposite nine. If number thirteen is missing, what number is opposite thirty?

7 How many digits from zero to nine have line symmetry or rotational symmetry greater than one but not both?

You will now need your Information Sheet

8 How long do the buses take to get from Brean Leisure Centre to the Royal Hospital?

9 How much would this carpet cost for a room with a floor area of fifteen square yards?

10 The commission earned is ten per cent of twenty-six thousand pounds. How much does the account manager earn in a year?

11 What is the size of the angle marked b?

12 The usual price for a standard staircase is five hundred and forty-six pounds. By how much is this staircase reduced in the sale?

13 What is the gradient of this line?

14 How much would VAT at fifteen per cent be on the six feet by four feet shed?

15 Write this number to the nearest ten thousand.

ANSWERS

1 20	6 63	11 100°
2 $\frac{1}{4}$	7 1 (or none,	12 £182
3 54 kg	discuss the	13 −2
4 205°	shape of 3)	14 £18.75
5 £2400	8 31 min	15 780 000
	9 £116.25	
	10 £14 400	

Extension 2

1 The mean of four numbers is five and a quarter. Three of the numbers are two, four and seven. What is the fourth number?

2 The perimeter of a square is four x. What is the area of the square in terms of x?

3 What is the next number in this series: ten, nine, seven, four, zero?

4 Write down the co-ordinates of the point one, four after a rotation of one hundred and eighty degrees about the origin.

5 How many seventy centilitre bottles can be filled from a barrel containing one hundred and fifty litres of wine?

6 In a test marked out of one hundred and twenty, a pupil scored eighty-four. Write this mark as a percentage.

7 Write the number nought point nought two seven six correct to two significant figures.

You will now need your Information Sheet

8 How much would it cost for a husband, wife and three children aged six, four and three to eat in the family restaurant if a ten per cent service charge is also added?

9 I want to build a twelve foot square patio using both sized slabs in vertical strips. Each size will cover the same area. How many of each type should I buy?

10 Last week a man travelled eighty miles at sixteen pence a mile. How much should he expect in his pay packet before tax?

11 What is the difference between the prices of the two types of windows after VAT has been included?

12 The price quoted is a twenty-five per cent reduction. What is the usual price, to the nearest penny?

13 The normal MGB exhaust costs twenty-four pounds sixty-seven pence. What would you feel to be a fair price for a Montego one point three stainless-steel exhaust under this special offer?

14 What fraction in its simplest form of the week's opening hours is Sunday?

15 What would be the average takings per hour if they took three thousand, nine hundred and twenty pounds last week?

ANSWERS

1 8	6 70%	11 £322
2 x^2	7 0.028	12 £3.47
3 −5	8 £24.64	13 £169.50
4 (−1, −4)	9 18 large,	14 $\frac{11}{149}$
5 214	32 small	15 £70
	10 £58.55	

Extension 3

1 There are nine point five French francs for every British pound. How much would an article cost in France if it cost nine pounds fifty pence in England?

2 Where does the straight line y equals two x minus three cross the y-axis?

3 The first direction to a yacht which is going to follow a square in a clockwise direction is north-east, ten kilometres. What are the next two instructions?

4 Using an approximate value of pi as three calculate the area of a sector of a circle of radius four centimetres with an angle of sixty degrees at the centre.

5 If one thousand pounds is invested at ten per cent compound interest, how many years will it be before that investment is worth two thousand pounds? Is it (a) five years, (b) ten years, (c) seven years or (d) two years?

6 Multiply the row matrix two, three by the column matrix two, three.

7 Counters are used to form patterns of the triangle numbers. Red counters are used for the first, blue for the second and green for the third. The counters are jumbled and placed in a bag. What is the probability that the first counter out is a blue one?

You will now need your Information Sheet

8 What is the total cost of three scooter tyres?

9 In only one year did the position of the company improve compared to the previous year. Which year was that?

10 Estimate the cost per hour of the Embassy snooker.

11 The cost of insulating a house is one hundred and eighty pounds. How much would someone with no existing insulation pay?

12 What fraction of the authorities used no microcomputers?

13 Estimate in what year the freight is likely to be twice as much as was carried in nineteen eighty-three.

14 How much would it cost to buy all three of the top fiction books?

15 What is the area in square centimetres of the smallest style B window?

ANSWERS

1 90.25 FF	6 (13)	11 £61.20
2 $y = -3$	7 $\frac{3}{10}$	12 $\frac{1667}{10\,000}$
3 South-east,	8 £25.95	13 1998±2 years
10 km and	9 1984−85	14 £32.85
South-west,	10 £3000	15 1849 cm²
10 km		
4 8 cm²		
5 (c)		

Extension 4

1 What is the square root of seventy-seven correct to the nearest whole number?

2 In the Falkland Islands' weather station the temperature one winter's day was recorded as twelve degrees below zero. The following day was seven point five degrees warmer. What temperature was it?

3 Three-fifths of a sum of money has to be written as a decimal fraction. What is it?

4 What is the surface area of a cube of side one point five centimetres?

5 If it is fine on any day in March the chances of the next day being fine is one in four. What is the probability of a day which is not fine following two consecutive fine days?

6 A paper boy is paid a half penny per day for every paper he delivers. He delivers eighty-four papers each day for six days. How much does he get paid?

7 The exchange rate is nine point five French francs for one pound. How much would the equivalent UK price be for a mathematical set which in France would cost twenty-eight francs fifty centimes?

You will now need your Information Sheet

8 I obtained a five per cent discount on the K registered Corniche. How much was that?

9 What are the modal digits appearing in the list?

10 What was the average (mean) number of Scouts for the three years?

11 How long does it take to get from the Butcher's Arms to Tesco's at Weston-super-Mare on a Friday?

12 The exhausts listed have to have VAT at fifteen per cent added. What is the total price for a Renault 5 exhaust in quality mild steel?

13 Estimate the month when the index first reached two thousand.

14 What percentage of the diagram is shaded?

15 What is the cost of the Bristol Channel chart plus fifteen per cent VAT correct to the nearest penny?

ANSWERS		
1 9	6 £2.52	11 35 min
2 −4.5°	7 £3	12 £37.95
3 0.6	8 £669.75	13 February 1988
4 13.5 cm^2	9 0 and 8	14 35%
5 $\frac{3}{4}$	10 421.3̇	15 £6.61

Extension 5

1 Two point six Swiss francs can be changed for one pound sterling. When I returned from my holiday I had sixty francs to change into sterling money. How much did I receive, to the nearest pound?

2 I walk two hundred metres in ninety seconds. How far will I walk each hour at this speed?

3 Posts are used to mark out a rectangle of sides six metres and four metres. How many posts will I need if the posts are placed two metres apart?

4 Which is the smallest, the mean, median or mode of the following list of numbers: two, four, five, six and six?

5 A line passes through the point zero, five with a gradient of two. What is its equation?

6 A bank uses compound interest each year to work out the money its customers have earned. I invest two hundred pounds for two years when the interest rate is ten per cent. How much interest do I get for the second year?

7 A network has three regions and six arcs. How many nodes will it have?

You will now need your Information Sheet

8 How much extra does it cost, before VAT is added, to have the smallest shed converted into a solar shed?

9 How long is the boat being used, for each day, between Folly Bridge and Iffley Lock?

10 What is the approximate percentage saving on the Relyon divan set?

11 The reduced rates allow one free lesson per person for every ten lessons paid for, if five or more people pay in advance at the same time. How much is saved if five people take up this offer of eleven lessons each?

12 A wages clerk gets an annual pay rise of fifty pounds in the first year and then one hundred and fifty pounds for each year up to the maximum salary. After how many years will the clerk be on the top pay rate?

13 For how long should you keep your lights on during this night time?

14 The Marlborough Consevatory is seven feet high. What is its volume in cubic feet?

15 What is the normal price of these suites if VAT is charged at fifteen per cent?

ANSWERS		
1 £23	6 £22	11 £35
2 8 km	7 5	12 4 years
3 10	8 £137	13 7 h 52 min
4 Mean	9 3 h 20 min	14 560 feet^3
5 $y = 2x + 5$	10 15%	15 £500.25

Test 1

1 What is the sum of the first five square numbers?

2 If the temperature at the North Pole is minus twenty-six degrees Fahrenheit and the temperature at the equator is eighty-six degrees Fahrenheit, what is the temperature difference?

3 What would be the height, to the nearest centimetre, of a cylinder whose radius is ten centimetres and whose volume is one-thousand, five hundred and seventy cubic centimetres? Use pi equals three point one four.

4 If a ship travels one thousand and eight nautical miles in two days, exactly what was its average speed in knots (nautical miles per hour)?

5 In a class of thirty pupils, sixteen do French, ten do German and six do both. How many do not study either subject?

6 What is the square root of twelve thousand, one hundred?

7 A meal costs twenty-four pounds plus a ten per cent service charge and then a further fifteen per cent VAT. What was the total cost of the meal?

You will now need your Information Sheet

8 Estimate the approximate ratio of the angles of this triangle, giving them in order, smallest first.

9 If the shop opens at nine a.m. during the week and eight a.m. on Saturdays, what fraction of the opening hours does Monday represent?

10 What is the percentage decrease in price of this packet of cereals, to the nearest whole number?

11 If I arrive at Bethnal Green station at one o'clock in the afternoon what time should I expect to get to Southbury?

12 Approximately how many months will it take to repay the loan on the car?

13 What was the approximate percentage saving on the Fiesta one point one Ghia?

14 What would be the total repayment, to the nearest one hundred pounds, of a loan of fifteen hundred pounds over four years?

15 Estimate the likely legal costs of selling a house worth two hundred thousand pounds.

ANSWERS

1 55	6 ±110	11 1347
2 112°F	7 £30.36	12 31–33 months
3 5 cm	8 1:2:3	13 7.5–9.5%
4 21 knots	9 $\frac{1}{6}$	14 £2100
5 10 pupils	10 11%	15 £1000

Test 2

1 A man swam thirty lengths in the public baths. He took a total of one thousand, three hundred and fifty strokes. How many strokes per length does this work out at?

2 The cost of a series of horse-riding lessons works out at one hundred pounds. Jenny pays three-eighths of the cost of the lessons, her father pays the balance. How much does each pay?

3 In a chess match the Russian Grand Master Oskavitz made a move on average every two and a half minutes. How long would he take to make thirty moves?

4 The total possible number of marks in a series of tests was six hundred and fifty. Angus scored fifty-eight per cent of the possible total. How many marks did he score?

5 The length of a rectangle is seventeen feet and its area is two hundred and twenty square feet. How wide is the rectangle?

6 In seven years' time Maria's grandmother will be four times as old as Maria, who is now eleven. How old is her grandmother now?

7 Divide three thousand and twenty-five by three and express your answer as a decimal number.

You will now need your Information Sheet

8 The total price is shared between five people. How much does each pay?

9 The temperature in Belgrade rises to eighty-two point five degrees Fahrenheit. How much percentage increase is this?

10 In the ski resort of Pec Pod Snezcou, what is the average length of each lift to the nearest metre?

11 You buy forty-eight English sweetcorn in packs. How much do you pay for them?

12 Robert owns one thousand shares. How much extra have they earned in nineteen eighty-seven as opposed to the previous year?

13 Three-eighths of the BP employees work in Great Britain. How many work in other countries?

14 The factory is working every day producing plastic drain pipe. How many feet does it produce in a fortnight?

15 In the last seven years the price of the Rover two one six Vitesse has increased by twenty-five per cent. How much did it cost seven years ago?

ANSWERS

1 45	6 65	11 £10.56
2 Jenny: £37.50	7 1008.33	12 £7
Father: £62.50	8 £195.35	13 75 000
3 75 min	9 10%	14 210 000 feet
4 377	10 756 m	15 £7474.40
5 13 feet		

Test 3

1 Thirty-nine Junior School children collect seven hundred and two leaves for a nature study display. On average how many leaves did each child collect?

2 r equals five, s equals eight, t equals six. What is r, multiplied by t squared and divided by s?

3 The new Chewitup chocolate bars sell at thirty-seven pence each. Alan bought thirteen. How much change did he get from a ten pound note?

4 Two trains start moving towards each other from stations which are two hundred and forty-five miles apart. One averages forty miles an hour, the other thirty miles an hour. How long will it be before they meet?

5 Deduct seventeen and two-thirds from twenty-six and seven-twelfths.

6 The pop group Havoc play five concerts. They are paid twelve thousand six hundred pounds altogether. There are three members in the group, who share the money in the ratio of one to two to three. How much does the middle member get for each concert?

7 Anna makes washers in a factory. She produces eight per minute. How many will she produce in six hours?

You will now need your Information Sheet

8 What is the cost of the tickets for ten children and two adults for a matinee performance on the sixteenth of January?

9 What is the mean (average) number of hours the pitch is open to the public in a week? Leave your answer as a fraction.

10 What is the range between the highest and lowest values attained during the period?

11 What is the cost of the smallest desk, a nest of tables, a dining table and a full set of six chairs?

12 Estimate the figure in pounds earned by the banks in nineteen eighty-six.

13 What is the mean (average) number of scientists doing pure research during the years nineteen eighty-three to nineteen eighty-five inclusive?

14 Give the operating profit as an approximate percentage of the income.

15 Which item offers the smallest percentage saving?

ANSWERS

1 18	6 £840	11 £647
2 90	7 2880	12 £2250m – £2350m
3 £5.19	8 £41.10	
4 3.5h	9 $2\frac{5}{14}$h	13 65700 – 80300
5 $8\frac{11}{12}$	10 $65 – $75	14 10%
		15 18 inch rope chain

Test 4

1 Give one factor of x squared minus twenty-five.

2 The sum of all the angles in a polygon is five hundred and forty degrees. What is the name of the polygon?

3 What is two cubed, multiplied by four to the power of minus two? Give your answer in decimal form.

4 Write down the inverse of the square matrix three, two, seven, five.

5 How many centimetres are there in one point seven kilometres?

6 A number written in standard form correct to three significant figures is seven point two three times ten to the power five. Write in decimal form the two numbers between which this number can lie.

7 Taking pi as three point one, work out the area of a circle whose diameter is eight centimetres.

You will now need your Information Sheet

8 For anyone buying five or more signet rings the price is reduced by thirty pence per ring. How much will Roscoe pay for eight rings?

9 Anne Coles was hoping to complete the marathon in three and three-quarter hours. By how many minutes and seconds did she beat this time?

10 A manager aged twenty-seven earns one twelfth of her annual salary in commission. How much are her total earnings for the year?

11 The Co-op pays a dividend of six pence in the pound on each quilt bought. Rebecca bought one of each type. To the nearest ten pence how much dividend did she receive?

12 How many cages for white leghorns were there in each block-long building?

13 Pierre bought a pair of jeans for sixteen pounds. How many French francs would he have paid for them?

14 Fourteen grouse lay the minimum number of eggs. Six lay the maximum number. How many do they lay altogether?

15 Queen Victoria was on the throne for sixty-four years. Osborne House was built eight years after she became queen. In which year did she die?

ANSWERS

1 (x – 5) or (x + 5)	6 723499 and 722500	11 £9.30
2 Pentagon		12 18000
3 0.5	7 49.6cm²	13 158.24FF
4 $\begin{pmatrix} 5 & -2 \\ -7 & 3 \end{pmatrix}$	8 £69.20	14 202
5 170000cm	9 16min 23s	15 1901
	10 £9750	

Test 5

1 The temperature in January is twelve degrees below what it usually is in April. The temperature in April is ten degrees. What is the temperature in January?

2 Which is the larger, two-fifths or nought point three three?

3 Estimate the square root of one hundred and seventy correct to the nearest whole number.

4 The radius of a pipe is to be trebled, how much larger will the area of cross-section be?

5 What is the surface area of a cuboid ten by five by three centimetres?

6 How many millimetres are there in one metre sixty centimetres?

7 A home worker is paid one pound per hour and one penny per letter addressed. How much is she paid for an eight hour day in which she addressed two hundred envelopes?

You will now need your Information Sheet

8 This is part of a bill from a French supermarket, how much is the total cost of the three postcards?

9 At what temperature is the expansion coefficient equal to one point five times ten to the minus six?

10 What is the probability of getting a number which has identical digits?

11 What will I pay when I order equipment valued at seven hundred and fifty pounds?

12 I bought the BSA motor cycle with ten per cent discount for cash. How much did I pay?

13 How much do two, one eight five by fourteen, eight ply tyres cost?

14 Write the money spent in nineteen eighty-one in figures.

15 What is the height in metres of the British Rail train from floor to the roof. (Use a ruler.)

ANSWERS		
1 $-2°$	6 1600 mm	11 £600
2 $\frac{2}{5}$	7 £10	12 £531
3 13	8 4.50 FF	13 £67.80
4 27	9 80–90 K	14 £7 200 000
5 190 cm²	10 $\frac{1}{4}$	15 2.55–3.05 m

Test 6

1 A batsman makes scores of sixty-one, twelve, twenty and thirty-three in four consecutive innings. What is his average score per innings?

2 There are fourteen pounds in a stone. What is the weight in pounds of a boy who weighs eight stone eleven pounds?

3 Write the next two numbers in this list: twenty-six, nineteen, twelve.

4 Add sixteen and a half to seven point seven five. Give your answer as a whole number and a fraction.

5 What is three q plus l cubed? l equals four and q equals six.

6 Fred earns eighty-six pounds a week. He gets a ten per cent rise. How much does he then earn?

7 Write fourteen million, seventy-thousand and six in figures.

You will now need your Information Sheet

8 What do I save by buying half a pig rather than a whole lamb if they both weigh fifty pounds?

9 A man takes advantage of this offer and travels one hundred miles during the first five days and two hundred miles during the next five. How many miles did he travel during the last five days to bring the average cost down to thirty pence per mile?

10 To convert Fahrenheit to Celsius you take away thirty-two and multiply by five-ninths. If Madrid were four degrees Fahrenheit warmer, what would the temperature be in degrees Celsius?

11 How much would thirteen of these volumes cost to the nearest penny?

12 A school organises a visit using the arrangements stated in this advertisement. If there are twenty free spaces on the fifty-three seater coach and the trip was priced at four pounds, how much money was collected?

13 What is the radius of this volcanic crater lake?

14 This line forms one side of a square on a map. If the map uses a scale of one to two thousand five hundred, what is the area of the square in reality using square metres?

15 What was the percentage increase in prescription charges between nineteen eighty-six and nineteen eighty-seven?

ANSWERS		
1 31.5	6 £94.60	11 £51.97
2 123 lb	7 14 070 006	12 £120
3 5 and -2	8 £7	13 0.75–0.85
4 $24\frac{1}{4}$	9 200 miles	miles
5 82	10 20°C	14 40 000–
		62 500 m²
		15 8.5–9.5%

Test 7

1 What is the reciprocal of four-fifths expressed as a decimal?

2 When seven hundred and fifty pounds is invested for one year it earns forty-five pounds interest. What is the annual interest rate?

3 Seven hundred and twenty people took part in a TV survey. Two hundred and seventy-three of them preferred BBC1. What size angle sector represents this group of people on a pie chart?

4 A bullet has a velocity of one hundred and twenty metres per second. How long does it take to reach a target four-fifths of a kilometre away?

5 What shape is a quadrilateral with all sides of equal length and no interior angle equal to ninety degrees?

6 What is the probability of getting no sixes when a die is rolled three times?

7 What is the sum of all the numbers in the fifth row of Pascal's triangle?

You will now need your Information Sheet

8 What is the price of one kilogram of yogurt?

9 The scale of this map is one centimetre to five kilometres. What area is covered by this map?

10 What is the product of the numbers of nodes, arcs and regions?

11 How much cheaper were one thousand units in eighty-six stroke seven compared with eighty-four stroke five?

12 What would be the monthly income on an investment of fifty-two thousand pounds?

13 This is part of a regular polygon. What is the sum of the interior angles?

14 Which of these letters have either one line of symmetry or rotational symmetry of order one?

15 What is the mean temperature in degrees Celsius of the first ten places?

ANSWERS

1 1.25	6 $\frac{125}{216}$	11 £1.65
2 6%	7 32	12 £455
3 136.5°	8 £1	13 540°
4 $6\frac{2}{3}$ s	9 225–400 km²	14 D and W
5 Rhombus	10 36	15 25.4°C

Test 8

1 Write the number seventeen point six five correct to two significant figures.

2 The average (mean) of three numbers is five, two of the numbers are two and six, what is the third?

3 Write four-fifths as a decimal fraction.

4 I buy pens at two pounds for twenty. If I make twenty per cent profit, for how much do I sell each pen?

5 Give the y co-ordinates of the point which lies on the line y equals two x plus one, which has an x co-ordinate of two.

6 A bicycle wheel has a radius of thirty centimetres. Taking pi as three give an approximate distance the bicycle travels forward in one revolution of the wheel.

7 What is the direction I must travel in to return home after an outward journey on a bearing of nought seven five degrees?

You will now need your Information Sheet

8 Give an approximation of the area in square feet of the second radiator on the list.

9 What is the cost of four coffees, two chocolates and three fruit juices? The prices are in sterling.

10 What is the percentage saving on the purchase of a Ferguson twenty-two G two, remote control television?

11 What is the cost of a trip to Cardiff for two adults and two children?

12 Make an estimate of the cost of fifteen metres of twenty-two millimetre copper tube, plus VAT at fifteen per cent.

13 In which quarter of which year was there the biggest change in the inflation rate?

14 What is the total cost of five, two nought five stroke seventy HR fourteen tyres?

15 What is the saving when buying seventy-five smoke alarms?

ANSWERS

1 18	6 180 cm	11 £16.90
2 7	7 225°	12 £24–£26
3 0.8	8 4 feet²	13 Last quarter 1986
4 12p	9 £4–£5	14 £258.75
5 5	10 13–16%	15 £487.50

Test 9

1 What is the square of nought point nought four?

2 Elaine buys three writing pads and receives fifty-nine pence change from two pounds. How many similar pads could she buy with five pounds?

3 After being reduced by twenty per cent in a sale a table is priced at seventy-two pounds. What was its pre-sale price?

4 Express seventy-six thousand, five hundred in standard form.

5 One sector on a pie chart represents one-fifth of the total information. How many degrees is this?

6 When five coins are tossed what is the probability of getting no heads?

7 How many lines of symmetry has a regular hexagon?

You will now need your Information Sheet

8 What percentage saving will you get on an advance booking for Monday the thirteenth?

9 Which of these letters have rotational symmetry order two?

10 Estimate the three figure bearing of Oxford from Reading?

11 What is the total current retail price including VAT?

12 Express the nineteen eighty-seven group turnover in standard form.

13 The scale of this map is one centimetre to one kilometre. Estimate the actual area that this map covers.

14 The owners accept an offer of two thousand, four hundred pounds less than the asking price. They repay their mortgage of twenty-eight thousand pounds and pay selling fees of four thousand, three hundred pounds. How much does this leave them with?

15 The company offer a further seven per cent reduction. Express the total reduction as a fully simplified fraction.

ANSWERS

1 0.0016	6 $\frac{1}{32}$	11 £4367.75
2 10	7 6	12 4.2208×10^9
3 £90	8 12.5%	13 20–30 km^2
4 7.65×10^4	9 I and S	14 £60 300
5 72°	10 330°–350°	15 $\frac{8}{25}$

Test 10

1 A motorist travels one point five miles in two minutes. What is his average speed in miles per hour?

2 A factory employs five hundred and forty people, of whom four-ninths are women. How many men does the factory employ?

3 Elaine buys eight copies of a book. She gave the shopkeeper thirty pounds and received two pounds fifty pence change, which was ten pence too much. How much was each book?

4 The reciprocal of a number is ten. What is the number?

5 How many discs of radius two centimetres can be cut from a rectangular piece of metal one metre by half a metre?

6 Concrete is made from gravel, sand and cement in the ratio of four to two to one, respectively. How much gravel is used to make four point two tonnes of concrete?

7 How many lines of symmetry does a right-angled isosceles triangle have?

You will now need your Information Sheet

8 To the nearest penny, how much is this corned beef per pound?

9 What was the mean height of the tides at the weekend?

10 Express the tangent of theta as a decimal.

11 What are the annual repayments on a seven thousand pound loan over five years?

12 A window frame is reduced by nine pounds and forty pence. What is its sale price?

13 Lines XY and YZ form two sides of a regular polygon. What is the sum of the interior angles of this polygon?

14 How much does each A-five leaflet cost to print?

15 Estimate the three figure bearing of C from A.

ANSWERS

1 45 m.p.h.	6 2.4 tonnes	11 £2019.16
2 300	7 1	12 £28.20
3 £4.70	8 £1	13 1800°
4 $\frac{1}{10}$	9 12.55 m	14 0.85p
5 300	10 1.33	15 325°–345°

Test 11

1 A restaurant bill of six pounds ninety pence includes VAT at fifteen per cent. What is the bill before VAT has been added?

2 Lucy devised an ingenious scheme to make one bar of chocolate last forever. She will eat half of what is left each day. What fraction will have been eaten after the first week?

3 A motor cycle can be bought for one thousand, five hundred pounds cash, or for a ten per cent deposit and twenty-four monthly payments of eighty-five pounds. What is the difference between the two methods of payment?

4 Write the number four hundred and seventy-six thousand and fifty-four in standard form correct to two significant figures.

5 Write down the fourth triangle number.

6 A piece of wire thirty-six centimetres long is bent and cut to form the edges of a regular tetrahedron. What is the length of each edge?

7 Three painters can cover the side of a warehouse in six days, how long would two men take to do the same work?

You will now need your Information Sheet

8 What is the modal temperature abroad in degrees Celsius?

9 What is the total cost of one twelve-inch Boss Hogg, one twelve-inch seafood special with extra prawns and two baked potatoes?

10 Estimate the approximate percentage fall in total staff from nineteen eighty-two until the end of the period shown.

11 What is the total amount repaid on a loan of ten thousand pounds for a period of ten years?

12 By what percentage is the aircraft quicker than the ferry? Give your answer to the nearest whole number.

13 What is the estimated percentage rise in the total world population from nineteen eighty-four to two thousand, one hundred? Answer to the nearest ten per cent.

14 Write down the time spent on the top three sports as a ratio to the time spent on the bottom three sports. Make any necessary approximations.

15 What is the total cost of an advert, including VAT, containing twenty average words?

ANSWERS		
1 £6	6 6 cm	11 £20254
2 $\frac{127}{128}$	7 9 days	12 133%
3 £690	8 33°C	13 110%
4 4.8×10^5	9 £10.85	14 18:1 – 22:1
5 10	10 20 – 30%	15 £54.63

Test 12

1 How many litres of water are required to fill a tank which measures two metres by one metre by one metre?

2 What is the product of six squared and negative three?

3 A sector with angle forty degrees is cut from a circle. What fraction of the circle is left?

4 The rateable value of a house is one hundred and fifty pounds. The annual rates payable are two hundred and twenty-five pounds. What is the rate levied for each pound?

5 What is the three figure bearing of London from the South Pole?

6 A box of forty-eight Mars Bars costs seven pounds twenty pence. Each Mars Bar is sold for nineteen pence. How much profit is made on each Mars Bar?

7 In a class of thirty-two children the probability of selecting a girl at random is nought point three seven five. How many boys are in the class?

You will now need your Information Sheet

8 How many grams of crisps does one get for one penny? Answer to the nearest gram.

9 Write the eighty-six stroke seven sales of units in standard form.

10 What is the cost of renting an Orion for one year excluding VAT?

11 How many pounds will nine hundred and sixty US dollars buy?

12 For what shape is this a net?

13 How much is saved when buying a three and three-quarter pound shoulder of lamb?

14 Estimate the three figure bearing of Bath from Trowbridge.

15 What is the size of angle c?

ANSWERS		
1 2000 l	6 4p	11 £600
2 −108	7 20	12 Cylinder
3 $\frac{8}{9}$	8 3 g	13 48 – 49p
4 £1.50	9 2.329×10^{11}	14 270° – 285°
5 000°	units	15 50°
	10 £2012.16	

Test 13

1 Antifreeze must be mixed with the cooling water to form a twenty-five per cent mixture. Write this as a ratio.

2 Mrs Williams measured the height of her window to fit curtains, it was seventy-one and a half inches and needed two lengths of material. What length of material should she buy to be sure of having enough, but not wasting too much? Give your answer in feet.

3 A single record revolves at forty-five revolutions per minute and an LP at thirty three and a third revolutions per minute. How many minutes of music to the nearest minute can be recorded on an LP using the same number of revolutions as a three minute song on a single?

4 A square-based pyramid has a height of six centimetres and volume of seventy-two cubic centimetres. What is the length of a side of the square base?

5 What is twenty-seven to the power of one-third?

6 Last night the temperature fell to minus nine point three degrees Celsius, which was one point six degrees colder than the previous night. What was the temperature then?

7 Mr Smith decided to decorate his wall with a mosaic of small coloured pentagons which he would fit together, i.e. tessellate. Can you offer him any advice on the best method?

You will now need your Information Sheet

8 What is the percentage saving on the Stonehill wall unit with table and four chairs?

9 Give this number correct to two significant figures.

10 Estimate the three figure bearing of Southampton from Ipswich.

11 Give the co-ordinates of A after a rotation of one hundred and eighty degrees about the origin.

12 What is the total number of lines of symmetry for these four letters?

13 Give the mean height of the morning tides correct to two decimal places.

14 A person makes a saving of twenty-seven pounds thirty pence. What was the sale price?

15 What is the size of angle c?

ANSWERS		
1 1:3	6 −7.7 °C	11 (3,1)
2 12–14 feet	7 Pentagons	12 2
3 4	don't	13 11.61 m
4 6 cm	tessellate	14 £109.20
5 3	8 $33\frac{1}{3}$%	15 70°
	9 870 000	
	10 230°–240°	

Test 14

1 Write the next two numbers in the sequence: one hundred, fifty, twenty-five, twelve and a half, six and a quarter.

2 Four people build a boat in two weeks. How many boats can two people build in twenty weeks?

3 Add four and a quarter to twelve and a third.

4 An antique is sold for two hundred and fifty pounds. It is then resold and a profit of five per cent is made on the original price. What is the re-sale price?

5 A coin is changed for four other coins. If these four coins are equal in value to the original coin was the original coin (a) a ten-pence coin, (b) a twenty-pence coin, (c) a fifty-pence coin, (d) a one-pound coin? Write down all of the possible answers.

6 q equals nine, l equals seven. What is q squared divided by l?

7 How far can you walk into a wood?

You will now need your Information Sheet

8 Express Others as a percentage of USA, as shown on this bar chart.

9 Given that one hundred and twenty-four thousand people are employed in services, how many people work in Hong Kong altogether?

10 Taking the mid-point of the group to be the average, estimate the total number of electorates in the thirty-one boroughs shown on the diagram.

11 Express as a fraction, in its simplified form, the cost of BMW twins with a round filter and an oil cooler against the BMW K one hundred.

12 This machine averages fifty miles to the gallon on petrol which costs one pound fifty per gallon. What is the cost of petrol used so far?

13 The total work force of British Columbia is seventeen million. What percentage are employed directly from timber?

14 What was the total population of Tibet in nineteen fifty-nine if there were twice as many males as females?

15 The price increased in nineteen eighty-three by fifty per cent to the prices shown. What was the lined two-piece suit price in nineteen eighty-three not including postage and packing?

ANSWERS		
1 $3\frac{1}{8}$ and $1\frac{9}{16}$	6 $11\frac{4}{7}$	11 $\frac{8}{9}$
2 5	7 Halfway	12 £808.47
3 $16\frac{7}{12}$	8 33%	13 0.005%
4 £262.50	9 200 000	14 720 000
5 (a), (b), (c)	10 23 250	15 £30
and (d)		

Test 15

1 A man buys a car for two thousand pounds and sells it for two thousand, five hundred pounds. What was his percentage profit?

2 A train leaves Liverpool at eleven twenty-seven hours and travels to Manchester thirty miles away, at an average speed of forty-five miles an hour. At what time does the train arrive?

3 The cost of one unit of electricity is four point five pence and the quarterly charge is four pounds. Mr Davis receives a quarterly electricity bill for forty pounds. How many units had he used?

4 In how many different ways can three people occupy three seats?

5 What is the square root of four-ninths?

6 The rateable value of a house is one hundred and forty pounds. The rate levied is two pounds ten pence in the pound. How much in rates does the owner of this house have to pay?

7 In covering a distance of half a kilometre, a wheel turns three hundred and twenty times. What is the approximate diameter of the wheel?

You will now need your Information Sheet

8 What is the cost of four thousand address labels?

9 How much can you spend if you agree to pay fifteen pounds a month?

10 Which bus should I catch to arrive at Axbridge by seven thirty p.m. from Locking?

11 In mid March how many Deutschmarks could be bought for one hundred dollars, approximately?

12 What is the average wage of employees in UK-owned companies in engineering, electronics and electrical industries?

13 The exchange rate is nine point five francs to the pound. Find the sterling equivalent of the change marked Rendu on the receipt.

14 The cost of insulation in my roof is expected to be two hundred pounds and for the walls two hundred and fifty pounds. How long will it take to get back my investment? I have electrical heating.

15 I invest twenty-five thousand pounds. How much will it be worth after two years. I do not withdraw the interest after the first year.

ANSWERS

1	25%	6	£294	11	186 – 188
2	12 07	7	0.4 – 0.6 m	12	£8000 – £9000
3	800	8	£14.24	13	£7.10
4	6	9	£360	14	3 – 4 years
5	$\pm\frac{2}{3}$	10	18 30	15	£29 160

Test 16

1 A journey of forty-eight miles took forty-five minutes. What was the average speed for this journey?

2 What is the cube root of negative one hundred and twenty-five?

3 In a group of people two-thirds are women and of these one-quarter wear glasses. What is the probability of picking at random a lady who wears glasses?

4 How many square tiles with edges of twenty centimetres are required to cover all the faces of a cube with a volume of eight cubic metres?

5 Seven hundred pounds are invested for two years. The rate of interest received is eight per cent per annum compounded. How much interest is earned during the second year?

6 The bearing of Bradford from Leeds is two hundred and eight degrees. What is the bearing of Leeds from Bradford?

7 One method of changing degrees centigrade into degrees Fahrenheit is to multiply by one point eight and then add thirty-two. Convert nine degrees centigrade into degrees Fahrenheit.

You will now need your Information Sheet

8 A square room has cost two hundred and twenty-five pounds to carpet using the middle priced carpet. What is the perimeter of the room?

9 The first customer of the day pays six pounds ninety pence for a tyre. How much has been saved?

10 What is the difference between the last two years' efficiency figures?

11 The test fee is eight per cent of the course fee. How much does the course and test cost altogether?

12 To the nearest month, how much older is Tucker than Tyson?

13 A man who will be thirty-one in three months time chooses Plan E. What will be his yearly payments?

14 What is the approximate percentage saving?

15 What is the size of angle y in degrees?

ANSWERS

1	64 m.p.h.	6	028°	11	£286.20
2	−5	7	48.2 °F	12	7 years 6 months
3	$\frac{1}{6}$	8	24 yards	13	£202.80
4	600	9	£16.10	14	13 – 16%
5	£60.48	10	0.43%	15	81°

Test 17

1 What is the surface area of a cube with a volume of sixty-four cubic centimetres?

2 What is the value of two raised to the power negative three?

3 Give the co-ordinates of the point three, four after a reflection in the line x equals one.

4 How much interest is received when four hundred pounds is invested for two years at seven per cent, compounded annually?

5 A swimming pool holds a quarter of a million litres of water when full. How long will it take to fill when water is supplied at the rate of forty litres per second? Give your answer in minutes and seconds.

6 How many lines of symmetry does an isosceles trapezium have?

7 What is the reciprocal of one and two-thirds?

You will now need your Information Sheet

8 The credit terms quoted are for two years. How much more is the credit price than the sale price?

9 What was the mean number of goals scored per match giving your answer correct to one decimal place? The figures in heavy black type are the number of goals scored so far this season by this team.

10 What is the ratio of Cantonese to Siyi people in Hong Kong, fully simplified?

11 Estimate the distance of Great Inagua from Miami.

12 How much of Hong Kong's invisible trade in nineteen seventy-nine came from tourism?

13 How much would a holiday in the Algarve cost for two adults and one child. (Children receive a twenty per cent reduction on the price shown.)

14 What is the size of the angle marked c?

15 By how much did the food production index rise from nineteen fifty-five to nineteen sixty-five?

ANSWERS		
1 96 cm^2	6 1	11 600–800 km
2 $\frac{1}{8}$	7 $\frac{3}{5}$	12 $6000–$7000
3 $(-1, 4)$	8 £14.05	13 £778.40
4 £57.96	9 2.4	14 75°
5 104 min 10 s	10 4:1	15 27–33

Test 18

1 The sides of the base of a square-based pyramid are doubled in size but the height is kept the same. By how much does the volume increase?

2 What decimal fraction is equivalent to three-eighths?

3 When multiplying two hundred and seventy-six by nought point three six on a calculator the string of numbers nine eight three six is obtained. Place the decimal point in the correct position.

4 The lengths of the two sides of a rectangular field are one hundred and twenty metres by sixty metres. Both lengths are correct to the nearest ten metres. What is the largest possible area of the field?

5 What is twenty-seven to the power of one-third?

6 What is the next number in the sequence one, eight, twenty-seven?

7 A man walks twelve kilometres north and sixteen kilometres west. How far is he directly from his starting point?

You will now need your Information Sheet

8 Explain the reason for the Cobalt bar being different from the others.

9 The nineteen eighty-seven, seven forty GLE saloon can be bought with a twenty per cent deposit. How much is that?

10 Estimate the length of the river Indus shown in the more detailed map.

11 In this survey taken some while ago three machines formed the bulk of the recommendations. What fraction of authorities recommended other machines? Fully simplify your answer.

12 What would be the cost of a set of five, one nine five stroke sixty HR times fifteen tyres?

13 What would be the cost of a Savoy bed if a five per cent discount was offered? Give your answer to the nearest pound.

14 What is the difference between the credit and cash prices?

15 What is the area in square feet of the aluminium foil on the roll?

ANSWERS		
1 4	6 64	11 $\frac{5}{34}$
2 0.375	7 20 km	12 £187.50
3 98.36	8 No new	13 £151
4 8125 or 7936 m^2	reserves	14 £266.59
5 3	found	15 222 feet^2
	9 £2599	
	10 500–600 miles	

Test 19

1 A speedway race consists of four laps. Neil won a speedway race in sixty-nine seconds. What was his average time for each lap?

2 Elaine bought a stereo system on hire purchase. Its sale price was three hundred and twenty pounds. She had to pay the sale price plus twenty per cent interest. How much did she pay?

3 Five people do a job in six months. How long would fifteen people take to do nine similar jobs?

4 q equals nine, l equals one, m equals eight. What is q squared times l squared plus two m?

5 What is four-elevenths divided by eight thirty-thirds? Give your answer in its simplest form.

6 The dearest tickets for a theatre performance cost twice as much as the other seats. A party went on a visit to the theatre. Half of them went into the cheaper seats at one pound fifty pence each. The tickets cost thirty-six pounds altogether. How many were in the party?

7 What is the cube root of one thousand, seven hundred and twenty-eight.

You will now need your Information Sheet

8 One-third of the people who enquired about the shares on one day each bought fifty shares. How many did they buy altogether?

9 What is the area of one of the back mats in square inches?

10 The Tefal Foodmaster costs twenty-six pounds. As a special offer its price is reduced by five per cent. How much would you pay for it then?

11 A rich man invests ten thousand pounds for his son. How much net interest does it earn in a year?

12 Elaine buys fifty scented polyanthus. She gives half of them to her parents and keeps fifteen for herself. She sells the rest to a friend at cost price. How much does she get for them?

13 You book a holiday on September the twentieth. You are taking your husband or wife to Rome on holiday three weeks later. You have put aside one thousand, one hundred pounds. After paying for the holiday how much will be left?

14 Your brother and yourself have to cancel your holiday to South India. The company gives you a ten per cent refund on its cost. How much have you and your brother lost?

15 The results of four of QPR's last five matches last year were nil–three, one–three, two–five and one–nil. What was the fifth result?

ANSWERS

1	17.25 s	6	16	11	£805
2	£384	7	12	12	£3.26
3	18 months	8	2 500 000	13	£474
4	97	9	253.5 inch²	14	£828
5	1½	10	£24.70	15	0 – 7

Test 20

1 What is the difference between the square root of eight thousand, one hundred and the square of thirty?

2 Roughly how many pints are there in ten litres?

3 What regular shape is needed to tesselate with regular octagons?

4 What angle has the same value in cosines and sines?

5 What is the largest area that can be enclosed in a rectangle of perimeter thirty-six metres?

6 A car wheel of radius forty centimetres rotates approximately how many times for each kilometre travelled?

7 Two round dinner plates are described as ten and a half inch and seven inch. How many times larger is the area of the bigger plate than that of the smaller?

You will now need your Information Sheet

8 How much more quickly does the nine eleven Turbo accelerate to one hundred miles per hour than the nine eleven Carrera?

9 Mr and Mrs Brown with two year old Karen and five year old James camp on the nights of August the fifteenth and sixteenth. They have a ten amp hook-up for their caravan. What is the total bill?

10 A checkout assistant at Gateway receives two pounds per hour on weekdays and time and a half on Saturday. What is the maximum he could earn in a week?

11 At the sale a family buys two pairs of swimming trunks, three check shirts, a Berkertex dress and two polycotton tops. How much did they save over normal prices?

12 Using the same rate of discount as on the Charnwood suite, calculate the saving on a four hundred and fifty pound settee.

13 The bag of organic fertilizer will cover sixty square metres. What is the cost of the number of bags I will need to cover an area fifteen metres by ten metres?

14 I need four new shock absorbers. What is the least they will cost me?

15 I have a fifty-four feet gap in a hedge. What will be the cost to fill it with four feet high panels and six feet high posts?

ANSWERS

1	810	6	350 – 450	11	£49.98
2	15 – 20 pints	7	2.25	12	£90
3	Square	8	3 s	13	£11.25
4	45°	9	£13.05	14	£72
5	81 m²	10	£125.50	15	£88.25

Test 21

1 Write the fraction three-eighths in standard form.

2 What is the surface area of a sphere of radius eight centimetres? Use three for pi.

3 Two of the sides of a right-angle triangle face south and west, and the angle that the hypotenuse makes with the side facing west is thirty-five degrees. What is the bearing of the hypotenuse from the corner with the south facing side?

4 A cube has a surface area of ninety-six square centimetres. What would be the volume of a larger cube whose sides are three times the length of this smaller cube?

5 How many planes of symmetry has a cuboid?

6 When seventeen pounds sterling can be exchanged for eight French francs, how many pounds and pence would you get for forty-four francs?

7 What number am I thinking of if sixty-five per cent of it is thirteen million?

You will now need your Information Sheet

8 How much will it cost for a family of a husband, wife and four children aged six, four, three and two to eat at this restaurant?

9 How much extra seed do I get by paying thirty-two pounds for one box weighing ten kilograms rather than spending the closest amount of money to this total on five-hundred gram boxes?

10 In what year would the number of primary school pupils approximately equal the number of secondary pupils?

11 What was the difference, in degrees Fahrenheit, between the hottest and coldest cities which had fog?

12 What is the difference between the savings on the two, five-door two-litre cars which run on petrol?

13 What would be the cost, to the nearest penny, of the cheapest insulation if VAT is charged at fifteen per cent and the owner gets a twenty-five per cent grant on the total bill?

14 Explain in a short sentence why the column for March does not add up to one hundred — give an example to prove your explanation.

15 What was the percentage reduction on the Relyon divan set, to the nearest whole number?

ANSWERS

1 3.75×10^{-1}	6 £93.50	11 16°
2 768 cm^2	7 20 million	12 £232
3 305° or 235°	8 £19.80	13 £30.19
4 1728 cm	9 500 g	14 Each per cent is rounded to nearest whole number, plus example
5 3	10 1988	
		15 15%

Test 22

1 Juliette buys three rolls at fifteen pence each and two cups of coffee. She pays with a pound coin and a fifty pence coin and is given thirty-five pence change. How much was a cup of coffee?

2 A bar of chocolate is cut into quarters and each quarter is halved. What percentage of the original bar is three of the smaller pieces?

3 Between which two whole numbers does the cube root of one hundred and twenty lie?

4 A cuboid is seven centimetres long, five centimetres wide and three centimetres high. What is its total surface area?

5 A salesman is paid one hundred pounds per week plus five per cent commission on sales. What value were his sales in a week when he earned three hundred and fifty pounds?

6 An aeroplane takes off at eleven thirty a.m. and flies at an average speed of six hundred miles an hour over a distance of two thousand, one hundred miles. It takes forty minutes to prepare the plane for the return flight. What is the earliest it can return?

7 Solve the equation x squared minus six equals nineteen.

You will now need your Information Sheet

8 What is the difference between the dearest and cheapest, fitted, reconditioned engines?

9 What is the final saving, when VAT at fifteen per cent is added to the price of this machine?

10 Approximately what fraction of a non-smoker's pay-out can a smoker expect to get?

11 If the firm pays three pounds per hour what would be the gross pay of this employee for his work on Thursday?

12 On what day is the difference between the morning and evening high tide the smallest?

13 What is the difference between the savings on the cheapest and dearest sale items?

14 In the last four years this house has risen in value by fifty per cent. What was its value four years ago if it is worth fifty-seven thousand pounds today?

15 What is the approximate percentage saving on this three-piece suite?

ANSWERS

1 35p	6 3:40 p.m.	11 £17.25
2 37.5%	7 x = ±5 (both needed)	12 Tuesday
3 4 and 5		13 £96
4 142 cm^2	8 £75	14 £38 000
5 £5000	9 £747.50	15 33–34%
	10 60–70%	

Test 23

1 The area of a right-angled triangle is thirty square centimetres. The hypotenuse is thirteen centimetres long and the base is five centimetres. How high is the triangle?

2 What is the value of eight raised to the power of minus two-thirds?

3 How many lines of symmetry does a regular heptagon have?

4 Twenty-four pots are spaced equally ten metres apart to form a rectangle whose length is twice as great as its width. What is the area of the rectangle?

5 What is the probability of picking one red bead out of a bag containing four red beads and three green if the first of your two selections is not replaced?

6 What is the equation of a straight line passing through the points three, five and five, one?

7 In the first ten matches of a season Everton averaged two point one goals per match. During the first fifteen games their average rose to two point six goals per match. How many goals did they score in the last five games they played?

You will now need your Information Sheet

8 What is the increase in opening hours, expressed as a fraction in its simplest form?

9 How many additional games would Saxon need to win in order to go above Crown in the league?

10 How much do I save by using two foot slabs rather than eighteen inch slabs in the riven finish to cover a rectangular patio eighteen feet long and six feet wide?

11 Using the information given, which do you think is most likely to be the true Brazilian unemployment rate: the EEC figures or the Brazilian embassy's?

12 These houses were all owned by one person, how much a month can he expect to receive if twenty-five per cent is given to the government in tax?

13 Which size of pellets offer the best discount?

14 A tray of thirty eggs is sold at two pounds, what would be the saving on buying five dozen eggs in trays rather than in half a dozen containers?

15 A kitchen is priced at four hundred and ninety pounds in this showroom, how much would you expect to find it for in other shops if this advert is to be believed?

ANSWERS

1 12 cm	6 $y = -2x + 11$	11 EEC
2 $\frac{1}{4}$	7 18	12 £1290
3 7	8 $\frac{1}{4}$	13 No. 2
4 3200 m²	9 3	14 80p
5 $\frac{4}{7}$	10 £12.15	15 £700

Test 24

1 The driver of a car notices that she passes the telegraph posts which are spaced at one hundred metre intervals every five seconds. At what speed, in kilometres per hour, is she travelling?

2 The floor of a four metre square room is divided into two parts. The centre part is formed by joining the mid-points of each adjacent wall to form another square. What is the total area of the remaining four triangles?

3 A model which is one-twelfth the size of a full scale yacht took half a litre of paint. How much would the full size yacht require?

4 A spinner is made so that each sector contains one of the factors of twelve. What is the probability of getting an odd number?

5 Estimate six point eight per cent of five thousand, six hundred and ninety-five pounds.

6 A man walks three times around a field which is in the shape of a pentagon. Through how many degrees has he turned?

7 What is one and a half divided by two-thirds?

You will now need your Information Sheet

8 What is the approximate percentage saving on the original price of the saw?

9 Estimate to the nearest five pence the cost per square foot of the six foot by five foot panel.

10 Estimate the likely level of productivity in nineteen eighty-eight/eighty-nine.

11 Which non-family standing ticket shows the biggest percentage saving if purchased before the seventeenth of July?

12 Write down the ratio of the amount borrowed to the total repayment for each of the period of repayments for one thousand pounds. Give your answers in the form of one to whatever, with the second figure given to one decimal place.

13 What is the average morning tide height to the nearest point one of a metre?

14 A discount of ten per cent is offered for total orders of over ten pounds weight. What is the total cost of five pounds of rainbow trout, ten pounds of haddock fillet and two pounds of peeled prawns?

15 What percentage increase does the Vanguard Trust offer over the full five year period?

ANSWERS

1 72 km/h	6 1080°	11 Under 11,
2 8 m²	7 $2\frac{1}{4}$	standing
3 72 litres	8 16–24%	12 *36 months 1:1.3*
4 $\frac{1}{3}$	9 25p or 26p	*60 months 1:1.5*
5 £380–£420	10 114	*90 months 1:1.8*
		13 10 m
		14 £25.88
		15 449.3%

Test 25

1. What is the approximate cost of twenty-one cakes at thirty-two pence each?

2. What is the next prime number after the square root of one hundred and sixty-nine?

3. A bag contains four white balls and six red balls. A ball is taken from the bag and put into a box. Another ball is taken from the bag. What is the probability that both of the removed balls are red?

4. It takes an hour and a quarter to mow a piece of parkland and another thirty-five minutes to trim the edges. It takes six minutes to check each piece of machinery and top up with fuel. What is the latest I can start in order to finish the job before lunch at one o'clock?

5. In this question b has the value minus three and c has the value minus two. What is the value of c squared minus two b?

6. One of the equal angles in an isosceles triangle is seventy degrees. What are the angles made in one corner by the line of symmetry?

7. Two hundred pounds is invested at five per cent compound interest for two years. How much does the investor have at the end of this period?

You will now need your Information Sheet

8. One thousand pounds is invested for one year in the Bristol Triple Bonus Account. What is the difference in interest earned between the net and gross rates?

9. What is the size in degrees of the slice allocated to Force?

10. VAT at fifteen per cent is added to the price the customer has to pay. What is the final price of a suite normally costing four hundred and eighty-six pounds?

11. I have a room fifteen feet wide and twenty-one feet long to cover with the most expensive carpet. If roll ends are available what can I expect to pay?

12. The manager is paid three pounds an hour on weekdays and time and a half on Saturday and Sunday. How much is he paid in one week?

13. How much would you expect to pay for a Vauxhall Viva clutch from this advertisement?

14. Work out **A** times **B**.

15. How many elements are there in the complement of M union P?

ANSWERS

1 £5.50–£6.50	6 20° each	11 £577.33
2 17	7 £220.50	12 £204
3 $\frac{1}{3}$	8 £27	13 £36.85
4 10:58 a.m.	9 36°	(assuming
5 10	10 £279.45	15% VAT)
		14 $\left(\begin{smallmatrix} 3 & 3 \\ 4 & 0 \end{smallmatrix}\right)$
		15 6

Extension 1

1. What is the reciprocal of one and three-quarters?

2. Write the co-ordinates of the point (one, four) after a rotation of ninety degrees anticlockwise about the origin.

3. The tangent of angle theta is three-quarters. What will be the sine of theta?

4. A rectangle is x centimetres wide and two centimetres longer. What is the area of this rectangle in terms of x?

5. When the radius of a circle is trebled by how many times is the area enlarged?

6. When four coins are tossed what is the probability of getting at least one head?

7. What is the determinant of the two by two matrix, one, five, two, one?

You will now need your Information Sheet

8. The distance of Sand Bay from Highbridge is twenty-four miles. What is the average speed of a bus travelling this route?

9. A room measuring six point five yards by four yards is carpeted using this carpet. How much does the carpet cost?

10. The commission earned is eight per cent of the turnover of twenty-six thousand pounds. How much does the account manager earn?

11. What is the size of the angle marked c?

12. In the sale a staircase costs four hundred and twenty-five pounds and twenty pence. What was the original price?

13. What is the equation of this line?

14. How much would the eight feet by six feet shed cost if VAT is an extra fifteen per cent?

15. Write this figure to one significant figure.

ANSWERS

1 $\frac{4}{7}$	6 $\frac{15}{16}$	11 50°
2 $(-4, 1)$	7 -9	12 £637.80
3 $\frac{3}{5}$	8 18 m.p.h.	13 $y = -2x + 2$
4 $x^2 + 2x$ or	9 £201.50	14 £178.25
$x(x + 2)$	10 £13 880	15 800 000
5 9		

Extension 2

1 One pound sterling is worth two point six Swiss francs and three point three Dutch guilders. When I changed one hundred and thirty Swiss francs into guilders how many did I get?

2 I run the four hundred metres in seventy-two seconds. What is my speed in kilometres per hour?

3 Posts are placed two metres apart to form a rectangle with an area of thirty-six square metres. What is the minimum number of posts I will need?

4 The mode of five whole numbers is six and the median is one smaller. The range is three, what is the mean?

5 What is the equation of a line which is parallel to the line three x minus two y equals seven and which passes through the point ten, nine?

6 The Cheshire Bank calculates its interest monthly. I invest two thousand, four hundred pounds for two months when the rate of interest is ten per cent per annum. How much money will I expect to earn, to the nearest penny, during the second month with compound interest?

7 A network has eighty-six arcs and twenty-three nodes. How many regions does it have?

You will now need your Information Sheet

8 How much would it cost for a husband, wife and three children aged from eleven to seven to eat in the family restaurant?

9 What is the minimum price for an order of lap fencing?

10 How many hours a year will this job be for, assuming you were allowed only two weekends off a year?

11 What would be the VAT you would have to pay on aluminium windows given the price quoted here and that VAT is charged at fifteen per cent?

12 How much a year will the rental be?

13 What is the difference in price between the cheapest and dearest types of exhausts which are not made of stainless steel?

14 For how many hours each weekend is this post office open?

15 Saturday assistants are hired at two pounds twenty an hour. How much a week do they earn?

ANSWERS

1 165 guilders	6 £20.17	11 £381.60
2 20 km/h	7 65	12 £135.20
3 12	8 £22.40	13 £62.50
4 4.8	9 £255	14 17
5 $y = \frac{3}{2}x - 6$	10 750 h	15 £15.40

Extension 3

1 There are nine point five francs to every pound sterling. What is the equivalent UK price for something which cost fifty-two francs twenty-five centimes?

2 The co-ordinates of a point which is on the curve y equals two x squared plus two is one, four. Give the y co-ordinate of the point for which x is three.

3 Give the next two directions for following a hexagonal course in a clockwise direction after ten kilometres on a bearing zero nine zero degrees.

4 Using an approximate value of pi as three, calculate the perimeter of a sector of a circle of radius four centimetres and with an angle of sixty degrees at the centre.

5 How long does it take for one hundred pounds to double if invested at ten per cent compound interest. Give your answer to the nearest year.

6 What is the result of multiplying the row matrix two, three by the column matrix two, three?

7 Counters are used to form patterns of the triangle numbers. Red counters are used for the first, blue for the second and green for the third. These counters are jumbled and placed in a bag. What is the probability that the first counter drawn out is either red or green?

You will now need your Information Sheet

8 What is the cost of two, eighteen inch trials tyres?

9 Estimate the average (mean) trading loss over the period of the graph.

10 Which of the top seven events seemed to have been the most costly per hour to stage?

11 The cost of insulating Mrs Sandhu's house, which has no insulation, is two hundred pounds. She is an OAP but does not get any rebates or supplementary pension. What grant will she get to the nearest penny?

12 Write the number of authorities using Apple II computers as a fraction of the total.

13 Estimate the year in which the number of passengers carried will be double those carried in nineteen eighty-three.

14 What is the mean cost of the top three paperback books?

15 What is the area in square metres of the largest style B windows?

ANSWERS

1 £5.50	6 (13)	11 £132
2 20	7 $\frac{7}{10}$	12 $\frac{4167}{10\,000}$
3 10 km at 150°	8 £27.74	13 2000–2004
and	9 £86 m – £100 m	14 £3.47
10 km at 210°	10 Natwest	15 0.8631 m²
4 8 cm	Cricket	
5 7 years		

Extension 4

1 What is the square root of four cubed?

2 The temperature on three consecutive days last winter was minus six point five degrees Celsius, zero degrees and plus one point five degrees. What was the average daily temperature?

3 What is sixty per cent written as a fraction in its lowest possible terms?

4 What is the total surface area of a solid cube of side two centimetres which has a square hole of side one centimetre bored from one face to the one directly opposite?

5 A submarine commander knows that he has a two in three chance of hitting a ship with a torpedo. He fires three torpedoes at his target, what is the probability of hitting with at least one?

6 A paper boy is paid a halfpenny each day for every paper delivered. He delivers seventy-five papers for the first three days and seventy-seven for the remaining three. How much does he get paid?

7 The exchange rate is nine point five French francs for one pound. How much to the nearest penny would a pack of four beers costing eighteen francs ninety centimes be in England?

You will now need your Information Sheet

8 I negotiated a discount of five per cent on the advertised price of the nineteen eighty-one Silver Spirit. How much did I have to pay for it?

9 What is the probability of drawing an odd digit from those appearing in the list?

10 What is the ratio of Scouters to Scouts in nineteen eighty-seven? Make a suitable approximation to obtain a simplified result.

11 How long does it take to get from Tickenham school to Old Church on a Wednesday?

12 VAT at fifteen per cent must be added to all prices. What is the total cost of a stainless-steel exhaust for a Porsche nine two four turbo?

13 What was the percentage rise in the index between the start of nineteen eighty-six and the end of July nineteen eighty-seven?

14 What percentage of the diagram is shaded?

15 I bought charts ten, twelve and seventeen. What is the total cost allowing five per cent discount?

ANSWERS

1 ± 8	6 £2.28	11 13 min
2 $-2.66°C$	7 £1.96	12 £249.55
3 $\frac{3}{5}$	8 £27 075	13 70%
4 $30\,cm^2$	9 $\frac{13}{29}$	14 35%
5 $\frac{26}{27}$	10 2:7	15 £17.10

Extension 5

1 How many different shapes form the net of a tetradedron?

2 What is the positive square root of two hundred and twenty-five?

3 How many two centimetre cubes would fit inside a four centimetre cube?

4 A ship leaves port facing south-west. What is its bearing?

5 Fifteen, one-pound coins stacked on top of each other measure fifty millimetres. How much would a stack eighteen metres tall be worth?

6 Houses are equally spaced on both sides of a street with even numbers on one side and odd on the other. Number one is opposite number two. What number is opposite number thirty-four?

7 How many digits from one to nine have at least one line of symmetry?

You will now need your Information Sheet

8 What is the final price per square foot for eighteen millimetre chipboard, to the nearest penny, assuming VAT is charged at fifteen per cent?

9 What fraction of the time is the Oxford to Abingdon boat moving during the working day? Give your answer using a numerator and denominator which are both smaller than twelve.

10 Which bed has the smallest percentage reduction on it?

11 When five or more people pay together every fourth lesson is charged at the first lesson rate. What would be the total bill for five people to have eight lessons each?

12 A VDU operator will reach the maximum salary after five years. The annual rise increases each year by ten pounds over the previous year. What is the wage of a person who is just starting their fourth year with the firm?

13 Each day in May the days get longer. Lighting up time is reduced by two minutes a day at both ends. What is the first day that you will be expected to keep your lights on for less than seven and a half hours?

14 The Highlight conservatory is seven feet high. It is made of glass on the two side walls, the front and the roof, which is flat. What is the total outer surface area of glass used?

15 What is the true difference between the reduced price and the normal price of these suites?

ANSWERS

1 1	6 33	11 £227.50
2 15	7 3 (or 2,	12 £4990
3 8	discuss the	13 12th May
4 135°	shape of 3)	14 276 feet²
5 £5400	8 8.25p	15 £271.40
	9 $\frac{9}{11}$	
	10 Relyon	
	Braemar	

Information Sheets

Q8

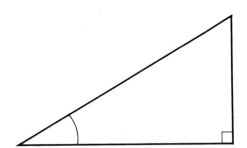

Q9

LATE NIGHT SHOPPING ALL WEEK	
8pm	Monday – Thursday
9pm	Later Friday
6pm	All Day Saturday

VISA   Access

Q10

Kellogg's Special
High protein rice and wheat cereal
FORTIFIED WITH VITAMINS AND IRON
LOW PRICE £1.08 **96p** 375g Pack

Q11

London Liverpool Street ⊖ 20A, 21 d	0833	0837	0849	0859	0911	—	—	—	0919	0929	0939	0949	0959	1009		1549	—	1555	1610	1619	—	1626	1650
Bethnal Green . . . . .20A, 21 d	0836	0840	0852	0902	0914	—	—	—	0922	0932	0942	0952	1002	1012		1552	—	1558	1613	1622	—	1632	—
Cambridge Heath . . . . d	0838	0842	0854	0904	0916	—	—	—	0924	0934	0944	0954	1004	1014		1554	—	1600	1615	1624	—	1634	—
London Fields § . . . . d	—	—	—	—	—	—	—	—	—	—	—	—	—	—		—	—	—	—	—	—	—	—
Hackney Downs. . . . . .20A, 21 d	0842	0846	0858	0908	0920	—	—	—	0928	0938	0948	0958	1008	1018	and at	1558	—	1604	1619	1628	—	1638	—
Rectory Road . . . . d	0844	0848	0900	0910	0922	—	—	—	0930	0940	0950	1000	1010	1020		1600	—	1606	1621	1630	—	1640	—
Stoke Newington . . . . d	0845	0849	0901	0911	0923	—	—	—	0931	0941	0951	1001	1011	1021	and same	1601	—	1607	1622	1631	—	1641	—
Stamford Hill . . . . d	0847	0851	0903	0913	0925	—	—	—	0933	0943	0953	1003	1013	1023		1603	—	1609	1624	1633	—	1643	—
Seven Sisters . . . . ⊖ d	0849	0853	0905	0915	0927	—	—	—	0935	0945	0955	1005	1015	1025	minutes	1605	—	1611	1627	1636	—	1646	—
Bruce Grove . . . . d	0851	0855	0907	0917	0929	—	—	—	0937	0947	0957	1007	1017	1027		1607	—	1613	1629	1638	—	1648	—
White Hart Lane . . . . d	0853	0857	0909	0919	0931	—	—	—	0939	0949	0959	1009	1019	1029	past	1609	—	1615	1631	1640	—	1650	—
Silver Street. . . . . d	0855	0859	0911	0921	0933	—	—	—	0941	0951	1001	1011	1021	1031		1611	—	1617	1633	1642	—	1652	—
Lower Edmonton . . . . d	0857	0901	0913	0923	0935	—	—	—	0943	0953	1003	1013	1023	1033	each	1613	—	1619	1635	1644	—	1654	1707
Bush Hill Park . . . . d	—	0904	—	0926	0938	—	—	—	—	0956	1006	—	1026	1036		—	—	1622	1637	—	—	1656	—
Enfield Town . . . . a	—	0906	—	0928	0940	—	—	—	—	0958	1008	—	1028	1038	hour until	—	—	1624	1640	—	—	1659	—
Southbury . . . . d	0901	—	0917	—	—	—	—	—	0947	—	—	1017	—	—		1617	—	—	—	1647	—	—	1711
Turkey Street . . . . d	0904	—	0920	—	—	—	—	—	0950	—	—	1020	—	—		1620	—	—	—	1650	—	—	1714
Theobalds Grove. . . . . d	0906	—	0922	—	—	—	—	—	0952	—	—	1022	—	—		1622	—	—	—	1653	—	—	1716
Cheshunt . . . . 21 a	0909	—	0926	—	—	—	—	—	0956	—	—	1026	—	—		1626	—	—	—	1657	—	—	1720

continued ▶

Q12

TYPICAL EXAMPLE	
NEW SUNNY 1.3 LX 3-door	
ON THE ROAD...............................	**£6950.00**
MINIMUM DEPOSIT CASH OR TRADE IN...............................	**£3000.00**
FINANCE CHARGES......................	**£365.50**
MONTHLY REPAYMENTS..........	**£136.02**
EQUIVALENT WEEKLY	**£31.39**
TOTAL CREDIT PRICE..................	**£4367.40**
YOU SAVE**	£1123.00

Q13

	NOW	WAS	SAVE
FIESTA XR2 Tints, alloys, sunroof	**£7095**	£7740	**£645**
FIESTA 1.1 Ghia	**£6163**	£6755	**£592**
FIESTA 1.4 Ghia	**£6605**	£7242	**£637**
FIESTA 1.4 S	**£6072**	£6655	**£583**
FIESTA 1.1 L	**£5506**	£6032	**£525**
FIESTA 1.1 Pop Plus	**£5132**	£5567	**£434**
FIESTA 950 Pop Plus	**£4895**	£5308	**£412**
FIESTA 950 Pop	**£4529**	£4828	**£298**

Q14

HOMEOWNER/ MORTGAGE PAYER LOANS

CENTRALISE YOUR COMMITMENTS. SETTLE YOUR H.P., CREDIT CARDS AND BANK LOANS, ETC, AND HAVE ONE EASY PAYMENT

NEW LOW! LOW! PRICES!

EXAMPLES OF SECURED LOANS, WEEKLY EQUIVALENTS

Borrow	36 mths	48 mths	60 mths	120 mths	Borrow	36 mths	60mths	90 mths	120 mths
1,500	12.41	10.06	8.68	6.10	5,000	40.68	28.18	22.22	19.47
2,500	20.68	16.77	14.46	10.17	7,500	61.02	42.27	33.33	29.21
4,000	33.09	26.83	23.14	16.28	10,000	81.41	56.36	44.45	38.94

TYPICAL EXAMPLE	TYPICAL EXAMPLE
£1,500×36 mths, £53.78 per mth Total cost £1,936.08	£7,500 × 120 mths, £126.27 per mth Total cost £15,189.19
APR 18.8%	APR 17.4%

CAR! HOLIDAY! HOME IMPROVEMENTS?. Specialists in Property Secured Lending. £200-£50,000 ANY PURPOSE

Phone or write in confidence for application form. Free Life Cover. Miras Loans. Early Settlements. Discounts. Local Rep can call on request.

Q15

CUT LEGAL COSTS
ON HOUSE SALE OR PURCHASE

EXAMPLE

PRICE	FEE
£15,000	£75
£25,000	£125
£35,000	£175

COUNCIL HOUSE PURCHASE — SPECIAL RATE £50

Plus usual Search and Land Register Fees
For details and specific quotations please ring
P. TIBBS
**Conveyancing Agent, Lypton Chambers
3 Upper Street, Crewe**

Book 5 ● Test 2

Q8

INTEREST FREE CREDIT
DEPOSIT £85.75.
PLUS 11 MONTHLY
PAYMENTS OF £81.00.
ROOM PRICE:
£976.75

Q9

Amsterdam	16C	61F
Athens......	31C	88F
Belgrade....	24C	75F
Bermuda...	28C	82F
Frankfurt...	19C	66F
Geneva......	22C	72F
Lisbon.......	33C	91F

Q10

Czechoslovakia GIANT MOUNTAINS
9 Days by coach £159

The most popular mountains in Bohemia offer superb facilities to all grades of skier and the resort of PEC POD SNEZCOU is well developed with terrain suitable for experts and beginners alike. 8 lifts totalling 6050m serve gentle slopes as well as long downhill runs.

Q11

HOME produced fresh chicken up to 3lb 15oz 69p a lb; 4lb 2oz frozen chicken £1.99 each; shoulder of pork 99p a lb; 7½ kg white potatoes £1.48(equal to 9p a lb); pack of 4 English sweetcorn 88p; French Golden Delicious apples 30p a lb loose, 29p a lb packs; 2 litres cola 65p; 4 x 1 litre orange juice £1.59.

Q12

First quarter results – three months to 30 June 1987
(unaudited)

	1987 £m	1986 £m
Turnover	2,407	2,252
Operating profit	633	573
Profit before taxation	561	502
Profit attributable to ordinary shareholders	347	304
Earnings per ordinary share	5.8p	5.1p

Q13

Soon the Government will be selling its remaining shares in BP.

It will be Britain's biggest share offer for Britain's biggest company. BP employs 120,000 people in some 70 different countries. Last year its sales were over £27 billion.

Q14

Today the two towering brothers—both are 6 feet 5—work 15,700 acres near Brawley in California's sun-flooded Imperial Valley. Their fields are half a mile square, and they raise cotton, canteloupe, lettuce, and other crops with tractor-plow combinations costing $65,000 apiece. And they've turned a melon shed into a factory producing 15,000 feet of flexible plastic drain pipe a day.

Q15

Gracefully designed, engineered for efficiency, the finely appointed Rover 213 arrives at a most civilised price of £7,196.
The 216 Vitesse at £9,343.

Q8

MAKE SURE OF YOUR
BEST SEAT THIS CHRISTMAS

Boxing Day,
Saturday 26 December
until Saturday 23 January

For
FOUR
GLORIOUS
WEEKS

P J PRODUCTIONS proudly present

MOTHER GOOSE

NOW BOOKING

A BEAUTIFUL, COLOURFUL,
PROFESSIONAL PANTOMIME
FOR ALL THE FAMILY

Performances:

Boxing Day	2.30, 5.30 and 8.30pm
Mon 28 Dec – Sat 2 Jan	Daily at 3pm and 7pm
Tue 5 Jan – Sat 9 Jan	Daily at 3pm and 7pm
Tue 12 Jan – Sat 16 Jan	Nightly at 7pm, Matinees 3pm, Wed. Thurs & Sat only
Tue 19 Jan – Sat 23 Jan	Tue-Fri Nightly at 7pm, Matinees Wed 3 pm Sat 2.30, 5.30 and 8.30pm

Tickets:

Boxing Day	All performances, all tickets £4.50 (No discounts)
All Saturday performances (except 8.30 pm)	All tickets £4.30, Children £3.25
All other performances	£3.50, £3.90, Children £3.25

10% DISCOUNT FOR PARTIES OF 10 OR MORE (Except Boxing Day)

Q9

UNIVERSITY OF BRISTOL'S NEW ARTIFICIAL PITCH

The University of Bristol is in the process of constructing a full-size artificial pitch
at its playing fields at Coombe Dingle which will be ready for use on September 1,
1987. Bristol City Council have entered into an agreement with the University over
the operation of this pitch in order to ensure its availability for public usage. It will
be available for public use at the following times:

Sunday Monday	11.30 a.m.-2.30 p.m. 10.00–noon	4.30 p.m.-6.00 p.m.
Tuesday		7.30 p.m.-9.30 p.m.
Wednesday		6.30 p.m.-9.30 p.m.
Friday		6.30 p.m.-9.30 p.m.
Saturday		5.00 p.m.-7.00 p.m.

*A full-size or a half-size pitch may be hired and whilst suitable for various sports,
it is envisaged that it will be of particular interest to hockey and soccer clubs.*

**Any clubs or individuals either interested in receiving further information or wishing to
make a booking should contact Mr. J. Browne, Parks Department, Colston House, Colston
Street, Bristol BS1 5AQ. Tel. 266031 ext. 524.**

Q10

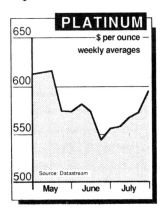

Q11

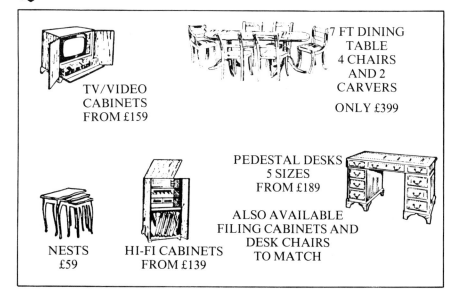

TV/VIDEO
CABINETS
FROM £159

7 FT DINING
TABLE
4 CHAIRS
AND 2
CARVERS

ONLY £399

PEDESTAL DESKS
5 SIZES
FROM £189

ALSO AVAILABLE
FILING CABINETS AND
DESK CHAIRS
TO MATCH

NESTS
£59

HI-FI CABINETS
FROM £139

continued ▶

Q12

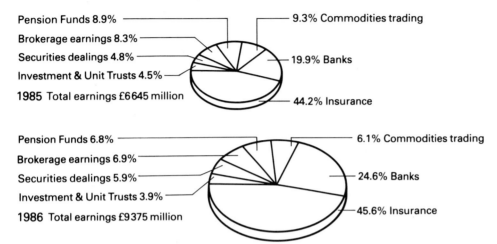

Overseas Earnings of UK Financial Institutions

Q13

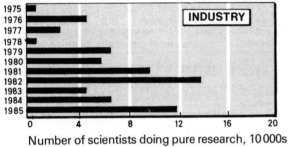

Number of scientists doing pure research, 10 000s

Q14

KEY STATISTICS	1986/87	CHANGE ON PREVIOUS YEAR
INCOME	£11,119m	+£376m
OPERATING PROFIT	£1,150m	+£206m
PROFIT AFTER INTEREST & TAXATION	£587m	+£173m
NET ASSETS	£37,066m	+£354m
UNITS SOLD (million kilowatt hours)	219,551	+6,273
CUSTOMERS	21,714,534	+227,593
EMPLOYEES	131,067	−399

Q15

Q8

£500,000 Stock Sale	
9ct Gold Chains from	£5.95
9ct Gold Bracelets from	£4.95
Signet Rings	£8.95
9ct Gold Earrings	£1.10
9ct Gold Diamond Rings	£13.95

Q9

Full Marathon: Derek Green (Abingdon) 2.30.07, Paul James (Weston) 2.35.06, Jeff Rees (Weston) 2.36.45. Ladies: Anne Coles (Washford) 3.28.37, Sarah Ayling (Axbridge) 3.52.21, Jane Betteridge (Westbury-sub-Mendip) 4.21.34.

Q10

Warehouse manager 21+ £7,500 p.a.
Warehouse assistant 19+ £5,720 p.a.
Manager 25+ £9,000 p.a. + commission.
Sales assistant 23+ £7,500 p.a. + commission.
Trainee sales assistant 16+ £5,000 p.a.

Q11

✱13·5 TOG HOLLOWFIBRE SEPARABLE QUILTS	Single	Double	King
CO-OP	£39·95	£49·95	£64·95
DEBENHAMS	49·99	69·99	83·99
HOUSE OF FRASER	44·99	69·99	79·99

Q12

With Ben Shames, Egg City's Executive Vice President, as my guide, I saw what that expansion has required: A mill to produce the 250 tons of feed a day needed for the craws of Egg City's layers. Two wells to supply a daily demand for 100,000 gallons of water. A packing plant that cleans, inspects, and packages a million eggs a day. Block-long buildings, each housing 90,000 White Leghorns, cooped five birds to a 16-by-18-inch cage, and with row after row of cages suspended three feet above the floor

Q13

£1.00 = 61.45 Belgian francs
9.89 French francs
3.33 Dutch guilders
2.96 German marks

Q14

Every bird species lays eggs of definite size, shape, color, and markings. There is, likewise, a rather definite clutch number for each species, from which they seldom depart. Auks and murres lay but a single egg; hummingbirds, 2; robins, 3 to 5; chickadees, 5 to 8; grouse, 8 to 15; and so forth. The number is probably an adaptation to the dangers to which the eggs and young are subjected.

Each egg has a definite incubation period, or time required for hatching. This ranges from the 10 days of a cowbird to the 78 days of a royal albatross, with the average around 12 or 14 days for small birds like robins and sparrows.

Q15

● OSBORNE HOUSE, WHIPPINGHAM CHURCH and PIRATE SHIP and EXHIBITION – Osborne House was built in 1845 as a country retreat for Queen Victoria. Apart from the treasures of the house itself, there are 450 acres of grounds, terraced gardens, fountains and a Swiss Cottage. Whippingham Church is approximately 2 miles away and has connections with Royalty. The Pirate Ship offers an under cover guided visit of a 160 year old vessel on the River Medina. See life-size pirates, parrots, music, sound, lighting and a visual exhibition. Worksheets available.

Q8

CARTE POSTAL	1.50
CARTE POSTAL	1.50
CARTE POSTAL	1.50
0005 EPICERIE	5.70
0005 EPICERIE	4.70
0005 EPICERIE	5.00
0572 VER/GOB	10.00
0005 EPICERIE	4.70
ORANGINA 1.5	7.45
0030 TRAITEUR	37.50
0070 BOULANG	4.20
0070 BOULANG	4.20
0005 EPICERIE	14.50
0050 CREMERIE	8.60
0050 CREMERIE	6.70
CONCOMBRE	3.90
0035 CHAR. TRA	5.40
0005 EPICERIE	7.90
0080 BOUCHERI	10.58
0080 BOUCHERI	9.33
0080 BOUCHERI	9.33
0080 BOUCHERI	9.33
S—T	263.12
ARTICL 32	
TOTAL	263.12

Q9

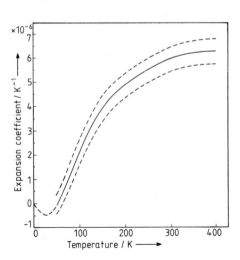

Q10

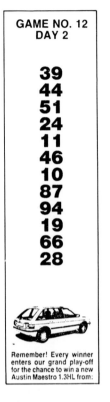

GAME NO. 12
DAY 2

39
44
51
24
11
46
10
87
94
19
66
28

Remember! Every winner enters our grand play-off for the chance to win a new Austin Maestro 1.3HL from:

Q11

SPECIAL INTRODUCTORY DISCOUNTS RIGHT ACROSS HYGENA'S RANGE OF KITCHENS

ORDER* VALUE	YOUR DISCOUNT
£65 – £124	£15
£125 – £249	£35
£250 – £499	£75
£500 – £999	£150
£1000 – £1499	£300
£1500 – £1999	£450
£2000 – £2499	£600

✳ Cabinets and worktops only. Offer ends September 2nd

continued ▶

Q12

BRADFORD MOTORCYCLES
All machines guaranteed and
M.O.T.d. No deposit terms.
Part exchange
Sample selection:
B.S.A. C15 250c.c.	£590
Y reg. SUZUKI GS125	£595
B reg. SUZUKI TS100	£595
B reg. SUZUKI GP100	£495
A reg. SUZUKI GP100	£435
B reg. SUZUKI TS100ER	£549
A reg. SUZUKI TS50	£495
Y reg. SUZUKI ZR50	£345
Y reg. SUZUKI FR50	£295
X reg. YAMAHA YB100	£325
Over 13 VESPAS	from only £295
Over 19 Mopeds	from only £125
B reg. HONDA MTX125	£790
A reg. HONDA XL125R	£629
A reg. HONDA MTX50	£439
X reg. HONDA MTX50	£245
A reg. HONDA Lead	£575
A reg. HONDA Lead80	£439
W reg. HONDA H100	£275
C reg. HONDA 90 Cub	£595
A reg. HONDA 90	£325
A reg. HONDA C70	£295
C reg. HONDA C70 Cub	£429
X reg. HONDA C70	£225
Y reg. HONDA C50	£275
HONDA ST70	£195
Y reg. HONDA CB125	£649
Y reg. HONDA CB100N	£395
V reg. HONDA CB250RS,	
Squires Sport Sidecar	£795

Accident and Repair Specialists
M.O.T. while you wait

Q13

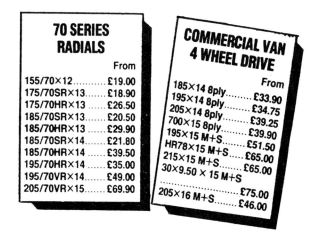

70 SERIES RADIALS

	From
155/70×12	£19.00
175/70SR×13	£18.90
175/70HR×13	£26.50
185/70SR×13	£20.50
185/70HR×13	£29.90
185/70SR×14	£21.80
185/70HR×14	£39.50
195/70HR×14	£35.00
195/70VR×14	£49.00
205/70VR×15	£69.90

COMMERCIAL VAN 4 WHEEL DRIVE

	From
185×14 8ply	£33.90
195×14 8ply	£34.75
205×14 8ply	£39.25
700×15 8ply	£39.90
195×15 M+S	£51.50
HR78×15 M+S	£65.00
215×15 M+S	£65.00
30×9.50 × 15 M+S	
205×16 M+S	£75.00
	£46.00

Q14

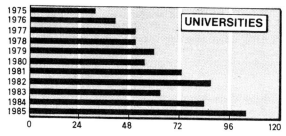

Money spent on research, × £100,000

Q15

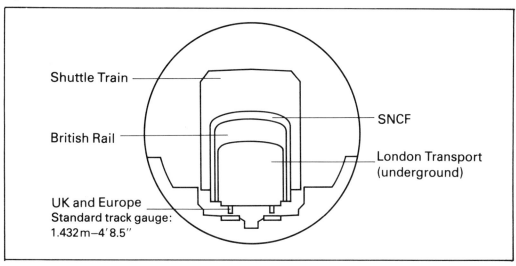

Q8

HOME FREEZER SPECIALS

½ or whole new season's
New Zealand Lamb ... **78p per lb**
½ or whole pig .... **64p per lb**
20lb pork tenderloin **£27.00**
(only £1.35 per lb)
Set 4 Ribs Roasting Beef
£1.08 per lb
Whole Rumps
Whole Sirloins·
£1.68 per lb

Whole Gammons
88p per lb

Q9

Aussiepass
unlimited travel
over Ansett Pioneers'
national coach network.
15 days about £150

Q10

ABROAD

	C	F	
Athens	13	55	Fair
Barcelona	16	61	Sunny
Brussels	10	50	Cloudy
Gibraltar	19	66	Sunny
L.Palmas	23	73	Fair
Madrid	18	64	Sunny
Majorca	15	59	Fair
Malta	14	57	Fair
Naples	18	64	Sunny
Paris	15	59	Fair

Q11

**All 20 volumes
of Children's Britannica
for just £79.95.**

Q12

On British coach tours allow one free place
per 8 paying members. As a special
concession we offer 6 free supervisory places
for parties of 47 because of 53-seater coach
size restrictions.

Q13

Near to Koblenz, Andernach is a charming
medieval town with a particularly interesting old
quarter and a beautiful 13th century church. You
can also visit the ruins of the town's original castle
which dates back to the 14th century and was
built to defend the entrance to the town. A visit to
the volcanic crater lake, the Laachersee, 5 miles in
circumference is well worth considering. There is
an indoor swimming pool and squash centre and a
children's playground.

Q14

Q15

HERE'S the rise and rise of prescription
charges:
1948. NHS introduced with free prescrip-
tions; 1952 One shilling (5p) charge per
form; 1961 Two shillings (10p) charge per
form; 1965 Charges abolished; 1968
Charges re-introduced at 2s 6d (12½p) per
item; 1971 20p per item; July 1979 45p per
item; 1980 70p per item; December 1980 £1
per item; 1982 £1.30 per item; 1983 £1.40
per item; 1984 £1.60 per item; 1985 £2 per
item; 1986 £2.20 per item; and now 1987
£2.40 per item.

Q8

~~£1.82~~
£1.49
Pack of 12 x 125g Pots
for the price of 10

Q9

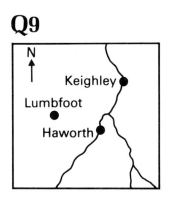

Q10

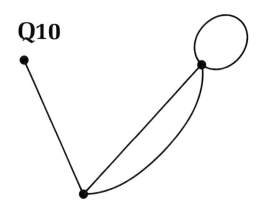

Q11

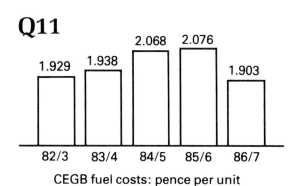

Q12

This is what 10·5% pa rate earns you every month					
INVESTMENT	AV. MONTHLY INCOME	INVESTMENT	AV. MONTHLY INCOME	INVESTMENT	AV. MONTHLY INCOME
£2,000	£17·50	£ 8,000	£ 70·00	£ 18,000	£157·50
£5,000	£43·75	£10,000	£ 87·50	£ 20,000	£175·00
£6,000	£52·50	£13,000	£113·75	£ 25,000	£218·75
£7,000	£61·25	£15,000	£131·25	£100,000	£875·00

Q13

a 72°

Q14

Q15

AROUND THE WORLD					
Lunch-time reports					
	C	F		C	F
Algiers	S	33 91	Lisbon	S	24 75
Amsterdam	S	21 70	London	F	20 68
Athens	F	27 81	Los Angeles	S	22 72
Barbados	F	30 86	Luxor	S	39 102
Barcelona	C	28 82	Madrid	S	30 86
Belfast	R	14 57	Malta	F	28 82
Belgrade	S	26 79	Melbourne	C	12 54
Berlin	S	25 77	Miami	C	31 88
Biarritz	C	21 70	Milan	F	26 79
Bombay	R	29 84	Moscow	C	23 73
Brussels	R	21 70	Nairobi	C	21 70
Budapest	S	24 75	New Delhi	F	32 90
Cairo	S	33 91	New York	C	23 73
Capetown	F	14 57	Nice	S	29 84
Casablanca	F	24 75	Oporto	F	20 68
Copenhagen	S	22 72	Palma	F	29 84
Corfu	S	28 82	Paris	F	21 70
Dublin	C	15 59	Perth	C	15 59
Dubrovnik	S	26 79	Prague	S	24 75
Edinburgh	C	15 59	Reykjavik	F	11 52
Faro	S	24 75	Rhodes	S	25 77
Florence	S	32 90	Rome	F	30 86
Funchal	C	24 75	Singapore	F	31 88
Geneva	C	21 70	Stockholm	R	17 63
Gibraltar	S	28 82	Sydney	S	22 72
Guernsey	F	17 63	Tel Aviv	S	30 86
Helsinki	C	15 59	Tenerife	F	27 81
Hongkong	C	31 88	Tokyo	C	26 79
Innsbruck	S	29 84	Toronto	F	18 64
Istanbul	R	20 68	Venice	S	26 79
Jersey	S	19 66	Vienna	S	24 75
Karachi	F	30 86	Wellington	R	10 50
S-sun, F-fair, C-cloud, R-rain, Th-thunder, Sn- snow					

Q8

Brugman Radiators guarantee 5 years with a superior smooth paint finish

PRICES START FROM £6.30

High	Length	Single Convector	Double Convector
23.6in.	18.9in.	9.47	19.81
23.6in.	25.2in.	12.58	25.83
23.6in.	31.5in.	15.71	31.82
23.6in.	37.8in.	18.84	37.81
23.6in.	44.1in.	21.95	43.80
23.6in.	50.4in.	25.08	49.77
23.6in.	56.7in.	28.19	55.78
23.6in.	63.0in.	31.32	61.75
23.6in.	69.3in.	34.45	67.76

Q9

BOISSONS NON ALCOOLISÉES / SOFT DRINKS			
Coca-Cola · Fanta · Banga Limonade · Tonic Water } Pression/Draught		25 cl	0.50
Ginger Ale · Bitter Lemon · BRITVIC · Boîte/Tin		17 cl	0.50
Jus de Fruits / Fruit Juice FRUIDAM · Bout. / Bottle Orange · Tomate · Ananas · Pamplemousse } Orange · Tomato · Pineapple · Grapefruit }		20 cl	0.60
EAU MINERALE / MINERAL WATER EVIAN		33 cl	0.40
PERRIER		20 cl	0.60
CAFE / COFFEE			**0.45**
THE / TEA			**0.40**
CHOCOLAT			**0.45**
CACAHUETES / PEANUTS			**0.40**

Q11

from BRISTOL

AVONMOUTH & PORTISHEAD

SAIL AWAY TO ILFRACOMBE — CHILDREN ONLY £2.50
SATURDAYS, AUGUST 1, 15 and 29
LEAVE BRISTOL 10 a.m., back 10.30 p.m. LEAVE PORTISHEAD 11 a.m., back 9.40 p.m.

Day trip to the seaside town of Penarth—OR *Cardiff—Capital City of Wales £5.95 OR stay aboard and sail on to visit Ilfracombe—glorious Devon £9.95 OR grand full day cruise — Welsh Coast — Exmoor Coast — and sailing on down the Devon Coast to Bull Point Lighthouse £12.95.
CHILDREN UNDER 16 — ONLY £2.50. SENIOR CITIZENS ONLY £5.95 — EVERYWHERE.

SATURDAY MORNINGS AUGUST 1, 15 and 29 LEAVE BRISTOL 10 a.m.
Sail through the Gorge and down the River Avon to Portishead. Single fare £2.95, children £1.95.

EVENING SHOWBOAT CRUISE
SATURDAY EVENINGS AUGUST 1, 15 and 29. LEAVE PORTISHEAD 9.40 p.m., back 11.30 p.m.
Evening cruise sailing up the River Avon through the Avon Gorge and under the Clifton Suspension Bridge, £3.95. ENTERTAINMENT ON BOARD: LOUNGE BARS, SUPPERS — why not make it a party?

SAIL AWAY TO ILFRACOMBE
SUNDAYS, AUGUST 2, 16 and 30 LEAVE PORTISHEAD 10.45 a.m., back 10.45 p.m.

Day trip to visit the sea-side town of Penarth — OR *Cardiff — Capital City of Wales £5.95 OR stay aboard and sail on down the Bristol Channel to Ilfracombe — glorious Devon £9.95 OR grand full day cruise — Welsh Coast — Exmoor Coast — and sailing on to Lundy Island cruising along the spectacular island coast £12.95.
CHILDREN UNDER 16 ONLY £2.50 EVERYWHERE.

STEAM RAILWAY TRIP — CHILDREN ONLY £2.50
MONDAYS, AUGUST 3 and 17 LEAVE AVONMOUTH 9 a.m., back 4.30 p.m.
Day trip to visit the seaside town of Penarth £5.95 OR stay aboard to cruise down the Bristol Channel calling at the West Country Harbour of Minehead £7.95 OR Cruise to Minehead — Steam Train Trip through the Somerset Countryside and 10 pretty village stations, coach trip through Somerset to Avonmouth. Inclusive fare £10.95.
CHILDREN UNDER 16 ONLY £2.50 EVERYWHERE, SENIOR CITIZENS — PENARTH £3.95 — CRUISE TO MINEHEAD £5.96 — CRUISE AND STEAM RAILWAY TRIP £7.95.

BE SURE OF YOUR TICKETS — BOOK NOW FROM Kiosks, High Street PORTISHEAD or CORSHAM, Whitemans Bookshop, 7 Orange Grove, Bath. ANY BRANCH of Bakers Dolphin travel. Tel. 213301 OR Book by ACCESS or VISA. Telephone 0446 720656 OR BUY YOUR TICKETS ON BOARD WHEN YOU SAIL.

On all sailings from Avonmouth — passengers should arrive at Port of Bristol Authority Buildings Free Car Park, St. Andrews Road, 39 minutes before sailing time to join the special free bus service to the Ship at the Dock entrance. *Cardiff is 15 minutes from Penarth Pier by regular bus service.

★ CENTRALLY HEATED LOUNGES ★

RESTAURANT · BUFFFET · BARS

Q10

For example:
HINARI CT4 14" Monitor Style Portable Colour TV SAVE £10 **£149·99**
SAMSUNG 347FA 14" Portable Colour TV 2 Year Guarantee SAVE £10 **£159·99**
HINARI CT5 14" Remote Control Colour TV SAVE £10 **£169·99**
PHILIPS 1014 14" Portable Colour TV SAVE £20 **£159·99**
HITACHI 1474 14" Portable Colour TV 2 Year Guarantee **£179·99**
SAMSUNG 340ZA 14" Remote Control Colour TV 2 Year Guarantee SAVE £10 **£179·99**
HITACHI 1476 14" Remote Control Colour TV 2 Year Guarantee SAVE £40 **£199·99**
JVC C140 14" Remote Control Colour TV **£229·99**
HITACHI 1646 16" Remote Control Colour TV 2 Year Guarantee SAVE £20 **£249·99**
SAMSUNG 515F 20" Monitor Style Colour TV 2 Year Guarantee SAVE £20 **£199·99**
PHILIPS 2036 20" Colour TV SAVE £50 **£219·99**
SAMSUNG 515ZA 20" Remote Control Colour TV 2 Year Guarantee SAVE £20 **£229·99**
HITACHI 2074 20" Colour TV 2 Year Guarantee SAVE £30 **£259·99**
PANASONIC 2061 20" Remote Control Colour TV 2 Year Guarantee SAVE £10 **£269·99**
SONY 2090 20" Colour TV **£299·99 ***
FERGUSON 22G1 22" Designer Colour TV SAVE £35 **£314·99**
TOSHIBA 211E 51cm FST Colour TV FREE 5 Year Guarantee SAVE £40 **£319·99**

FERGUSON 22G2 22" Remote Control Designer Colour TV SAVE £55 **£344·99**
SONY 2215 22" Remote Control Colour TV SAVE £30 **£369·99 ***
TOSHIBA 212R 51cm Remote Control FST Colour TV FREE 5 Year Guarantee SAVE £10 **£369·99**
TOSHIBA 213R 51cm Remote Control FST Colour TV FREE 5 Year Guarantee SAVE £10 **£369·99**
PANASONIC TX1 51cm Teletext Colour TV 2 Year Guarantee **£399·99**
SONY 2096 20" Teletext Colour TV **£399·99 ***
SONY 2217 22" Teletext Colour TV SAVE £50 **£399·99 ***
HITACHI 2178 51cm Teletext Colour TV 2 Year Guarantee SAVE £50 **£429·99**
TOSHIBA 211T 51cm Stereo Teletext Colour TV FREE 5 Year Guarantee SAVE £20 **£479·99**
TOSHIBA 213D 51cm Stereo Teletext Colour TV FREE 5 Year Guarantee SAVE £20 **£479·99**
VIDEO
SAMSUNG 616T Infra-Red Remote Control VHS Video SAVE £70 **£269·99**
AMSTRAD 4600 Long Play VHS Video SAVE £30 **£299·99**
PHILIPS 6542 Infra-Red Remote Control VHS Video SAVE £50 **£349·99**
HITACHI VT220 Remote Control Programmable VHS Video SAVE £30 **£369·99**
PANASONIC NVG12 Slimline Remote Control Programmable VHS Video **£399·99**
PANASONIC NVG21 Digital Scan Programming VHS Video **£449·99**

continued ▶

Q12

15mm Copper Tube	73p per metre
22mm Copper Tube	£1.45 per metre
28mm Copper Tube	£1.78 per metre

Q13

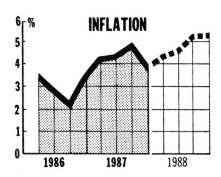

Q14

HIGH PERFORMANCE TYRES

LIFETIME MILEAGE GUARANTEE

"60" SERIES Low Profile 'H' rated.		"70" SERIES 'H' rated.	
Size	Kwik-Fit Price From	Size	Kwik-Fit Price From
185/60 HR 13	£**33**.00 +£4.95 +VAT	185/70 HR 13	£**35**.00 +£5.25 +VAT
185/60 HR 14	£**38**.00 +£5.70	185/70 HR 14	£**35**.00 +£5.25
		195/70 HR 14	£**39**.00 +£5.85
195/60 HR 14	£**42**.00 +£6.30	205/70 HR 14	£**45**.00 +£6.75

Q15

DISHWASHERS
12 place settings 6 programmes Normally £219.95 £**179**.95

'Colonist' PANELLED LOOK INTERNAL DOORS
Primed ready for finishing 78in. x 30in. Normally £34.95. £**24**.95

Heavy Duty CONTRACTORS WHEELBARROWS
with pneumatic tyre and tube Normally £19.95 £**16**.95

INDESIT AUTOMATIC WASHING MACHINES
600/800 spin speed Hot & Cold fill £**189**.95

CRISTAL CERAMIC TILE SCOOP
Huge selection, slight subs **10**p per tile

BLACK & DECKER SMOKE ALARMS
R.R.P. £16.45 £**9**.95

HINGED BATH SHOWER SCREENS
Aluminium frame, perspex panel Normally £29.95 £**19**.95

Q8

10th·WORLD·WINE·FAIR

Sponsored by Bristol City Council and JT Group

•ADVANCE BOOKING FORM•

Final date for receipt of Booking Form is June 26

JULY	NORMAL PRICE	ADVANCE BOOKING PRICE	NO. OF TICKETS REQ.	PARTIES OVER 20	NO. OF TICKETS REQ.	TOTAL £
FRIDAY 10th 11am-4pm	£4.00	**£3.50**		£3.00		
FRIDAY 10th 6pm-10pm	£6.50	**£6.00**		£5.50		
SATURDAY 11th 11am-4pm	£5.50	**£5.00**		£4.50		
SATURDAY 11th 6pm-10pm	£6.50	**£6.00**		£5.50		
SUNDAY 12th 12-6pm	£6.50	**£6.00**		£5.50		
MONDAY 13th 11am-4pm	£4.00	**£3.50**		£3.00		

Q9

Q10

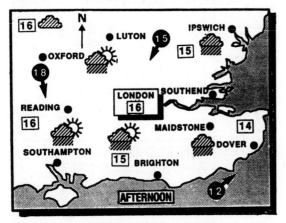

continued ▶

Q11

> # METRO 1.0 310 City Van
> ## 86 (D) registered but unused
> Still under manufacturers warranty
> Current Retail Price (new)…£3885 + **VAT @ 15%**
> **OUR PRICE**………………**£3200** + **VAT@15%**

Q12

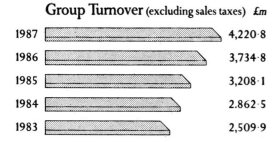

Group Turnover (excluding sales taxes) *£m*

1987	4,220·8
1986	3,734·8
1985	3,208·1
1984	2.862·5
1983	2,509·9

Q13

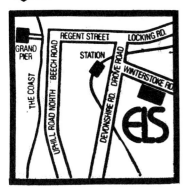

Q14

SUPERB RESIDENCE

Central address, easy reach sea front, etc. Individual residence. Ideal family. Cloaks., 2 exc. recs., spac. b'fast/kit., 4 beds. Pleasant sunny gdns., garage, exc. caravan space.
£95,000

Q15

> # DUNLOPILLO
> # DIVAN SETS LESS **25%**

Q8

.85p
79P 12oz Can

Q9

Tide Times
British Summer Time

August

	am	m	pm	m
Thurs 6	04.04	10.4	16.43	10.8
Fri 7	05.20	11.0	18.00	11.6
Sat 8	06.35	11.9	19.03	12.5
Sun 9	07.34	12.6	19.56	13.2
Mon 10	08.23	13.2	20.43	13.7
Tues 11	09.08	13.5	21.25	13.9
Wed 12	09.49	13.6	22.06	13.8

Q11

ANY PURPOSE HOMEOWNER/ MORTGAGE PAYER LOANS
NO FEES
Weekly equivalent repayments to nearest penny over

BORROW	180 Mths £	120 Mths £	96 Mths £	60 Mths £	A.P.R.
£15,000	48.07	55.50	61.80	82.06	**15.8%**
£10,000	32.04	37.00	41.19	54.70	
BORROW	144 Mths £	120 Mths £	90 Mths £	60 Mths £	A.P.R.
£8,500	29.44	31.64	36.42	46.66	**16.0%**
£7,500	25.97	27.92	32.14	41.17	
BORROW	180 Mths £	120 Mths £	84 Mths £	60 Mths £	A.P.R.
£7,000	23.14	26.53	31.60	38.83	**16.6%**
£6,000	19.83	22.74	27.09	33.29	
£5,500	18.18	20.85	24.83	30.51	
BORROW	120 Mths £	84 Mths £	60 Mths £	36 Mths £	A.P.R.
£4,750	18.35	21.76	26.64	38.52	**17.2%**
£4,500	17.38	20.61	25.24	36.50	
£4,250	16.41	19.47	23.84	34.47	
BORROW	120 Mths £	84 Mths £	60 Mths £	36 Mths £	A.P.R.
£3,750	14.60	16.66	21.13	30.51	**17.4%**
£3,500	13.63	15.55	19.72	28.47	
BORROW	120 Mths £	84 Mths £	60 Mths £	36 Mths £	A.P.R.
£3,250	12.82	15.13	18.46	26.57	**17.8%**
£3,000	11.84	13.97	17.04	24.53	
£2,500	9.86	11.64	14.20	20.44	
BORROW	120 Mths £	90 Mths £	60 Mths £	36 Mths £	A.P.R.
£1,750	7.12	8.06	10.12	14.48	**18.8%**
£1,500	6.10	6.91	8.67	12.41	
£1,000	4.07	4.60	5.78	8.27	

Typical example: Borrow £1,000 over 36 mths at £35.85 per mth = £1,290.60 total repaid. APR 18.8%

Q10

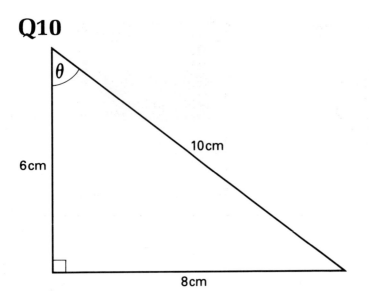

continued ▶

Q12

- 18in x 18in PATIO PAVING SLABS **£1.06** + **VAT**
- 5 LITRE TINS VINYL SILK **£6.95** + **VAT**
- 6ft x 6ft FENCE PANELS — TREATED LAP **£9.79** + **VAT**
- **25%** OFF JOHN CARR DOORS AND WINDOW FRAMES
- **30%** OFF BRASS IRONMONGERY
- **30%** OFF BARTOL PLASTICS

Q13

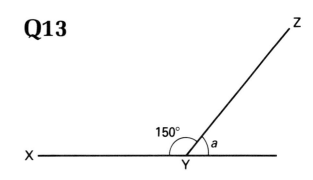

Q14

A5 LEAFLETS 1 colour, 1 side...... **£8.50** 1000
A4 LEAFLETS 1 colour, 1 side........... **£15** 1000
MINIMUM ORDER 5000

Q15

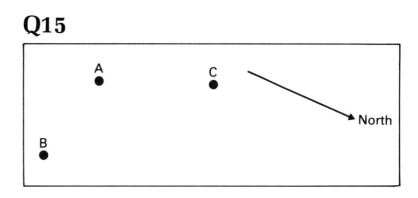

Q8

AT HOME . . .

Bournemouth	23C	73F	bright	Ilfracombe	19C 66F	sunny
Bridlington	18C	64F	sunny	Jersey	25C 77F	sunny
Bristol	25C	77F	sunny	London	24C 75F	sunny
Carlisle	20C	68F	drizzle	Newquay	22C 72F	sunny
Colwyn Bay	23C	73F	sunny	Scarboro'	17C 63F	sunny
Cromer	20C	68F	sunny	Tenby	19C 66F	sunny
Dublin	21C	70F	clear	Torquay	22C 72F	sunny
Edinburgh	20C	68F	drizzle	Weston	25C 77F	sunny

. . . AND ABROAD

Amsterdam	20C	68F	cloudy	Madrid	33C 91F	cloudy
Athens	33C	91F	clear	Moscow	17C 63F	cloudy
Belgrade	30C	86F	clear	New York	31C 88F	cloudy
Bermuda	26C	80F	clear	Nicosia	36C 97F	clear
Frankfurt	25C	77F	cloudy	Paris	26C 79F	clear
Geneva	27C	81F	clear	Rome	33C 91F	clear
Lisbon	25C	77F	clear	Stockholm	18C 64F	cloudy

Q9

PIZZA DELIVERY SERVICE
MENU

	9"	12"	14"
CHEESE & TOMATO Our basic pizza made with our own homemade pizza base topped with tomatoes and mozzarella cheese.	1.85	2.75	3.25
MEXICAN CHILLI Our pizza base smothered in a spicy and meaty chilli sauce and topped with mozzarella cheese	2.75	3.75	4.75
SEAFOOD SPECIAL Deep sea prawns, crab meat and chunks of cod in a provencale sauce on our pizza base and topped with mozzarella cheese.	3.25	4.25	5.25
HAWAIIAN Chunks of pineapple and strips of tasty mild cured ham on our pizza base and topped with mozzarella cheese	2.60	3.60	4.50
SPICY VEGETARIAN Fresh chunky vegetables including onions, courgettes, mushrooms, tomatoes, aubergines, peppers and garlic in a spicy curry sauce, topped with mozzarella on a wholemeal pizza base.	2.60	3.50	4.25
BOSS HOGG Our gluttenous special, a pizza so full of prawns, pepperoni, mushrooms, salami, peppers, tomatoes and mozzarella cheese that it is sure to satisfy the biggest appetite.	3.65	5.00	6.25

GARLIC BREAD 65p   **BAKED POTATO** 45p

EXTRA TOPPINGS

	9"	12"	14"		9"	12"	14"		9"	12"	14"
A Ham	40	50	60	E Anchovies	50	60	70	I Olives	25	35	45
B Salami	40	50	60	F Onions	20	30	40	J Garlic	25	35	45
C Pepperoni	40	50	60	G Mushrooms	45	60	75	K Pineapple	35	45	65
D Prawns	60	70	80	H Peppers	20	30	40	L Cheese	50	60	70

Q10

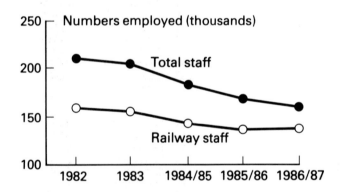

Numbers employed (thousands)

Total staff

Railway staff

250 — 200 — 150 — 100

1982   1983   1984/85   1985/86   1986/87

Q11

Typical Equivalent. Weekly cost status loans					APR%
PHONE US NOW FOR IMMEDIATE ACTION	**AMOUNT £2,000**	**3 YEARS £16.54**	**5 YEARS £11.57**	**10 YEARS £8.13**	**15 YEARS N/A**
	£4,000	£33.09	£23.14	£16.27	N/A	18.8
	£6,000	£49.64	£34.71	£24.41	£21.70	
	£10,000	£81.14	£55.37	£38.95	£34.22	17.4

continued ▶

Q12

London-Paris Passenger Times (city centre to city centre)

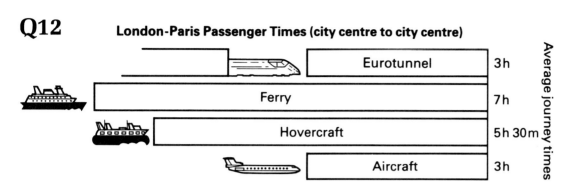

Eurotunnel	3h
Ferry	7h
Hovercraft	5h 30m
Aircraft	3h

Average journey times

Q13

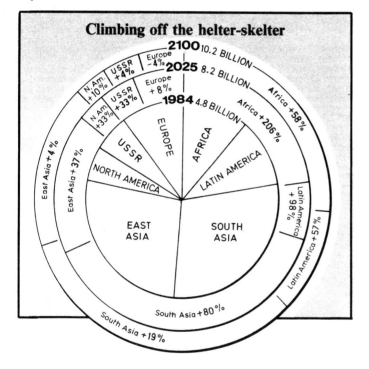

Climbing off the helter-skelter

2100 — 10.2 BILLION
2025 — 8.2 BILLION
1984 — 4.8 BILLION

Europe −4%
Europe +8%
USSR +4%
USSR +33%
N. Am. +10%
N. Am. +33%
Africa +58%
Africa +206%
Latin America +98%
Latin America +57%
East Asia +4%
East Asia +37%
South Asia +80%
South Asia +19%

EUROPE
AFRICA
USSR
NORTH AMERICA
LATIN AMERICA
EAST ASIA
SOUTH ASIA

Q14

	TOP 20 SPORTS ON TV, 1986	
	Sport	**Hrs/mins**
1	Snooker	394/11
2	Cricket	335/41
3	Horse racing	275/54
4	Soccer	262/00[1]
5	Tennis	188/52
6	Golf	148/59
7	Athletics	131/04[2]
8	Bowls	112/00
9	Boxing	58/57
10	Equestrian	56/41
11	Darts	54/10
12	Wrestling	43/00
13	Motor racing	41/32
14	Ice skating	40/57
15	Rugby union	39/50
16	Cycling	27/20
17	Rugby league	21/09
18	Gymnastics	18/50
19	Motor cycling	17/51
20	Yachting	16/40

[1] inc world cup [2] inc European championship

Q15

PUT YOUR PROPERTY ON THE SUNDAY MARKET

To advertise in The Sunday Times Classified, fill in your advertisement in the space below. (Longer messages can be attached separately). Rates are: £9.50 per line (approximately four words, minimum three lines) £56.00 per s.c.c. full display. Plus 15% VAT.

Q8

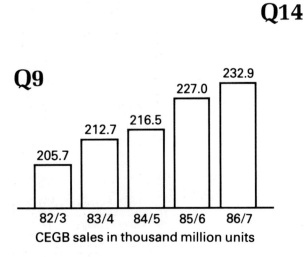

59P

Pack of 7 x 25g Bags
for the price of 6

I BAG EXTRA **FREE**
7 FOR THE NORMAL PRICE OF 6

TESCO

CRISPS

• CHEESE & ONION FLAVOUR •

6 7

Q12

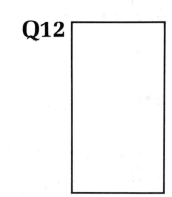

Q13

Farmhouse Cheddar Cheese (loose from the provisions counter) ~~£1.46~~	**£1.29**
Fresh British Shoulder of Lamb Per lb ~~99p~~	**86**P
Tesco Spanish Table Wine 70cl Bottle ~~£1.69~~	**£1.59**
Tesco Pear Quarters in Syrup 410g Can ~~37p~~	**32**P

Q9

205.7 212.7 216.5 227.0 232.9

82/3 83/4 84/5 85/6 86/7

CEGB sales in thousand million units

Q14

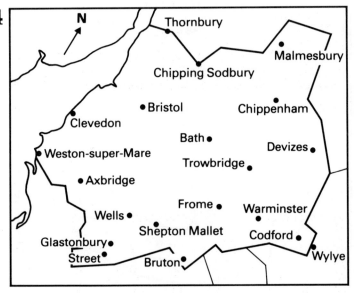

N

Thornbury
Malmesbury
Chipping Sodbury
Chippenham
Bristol
Clevedon
Bath
Devizes
Weston-super-Mare
Trowbridge
Axbridge
Frome Warminster
Wells
Codford
Shepton Mallet
Glastonbury
Street Bruton Wylye

Q10

LEASING

NEVER KNOWINGLY UNDERSOLD
ON TOTAL CONTRACT COST

Fiesta 1,100L. £139.75
Escort 1.4L 5 dr.:.......... £164.71
Orion 1400L. £167.68
Sapphire 1800L. £183.53
Sierra 1800L. £186.29
Granada 2.0 EFi GL. £273.84

The above monthly rentals relate to a four-year flexible lease and are subject to V.A.T. Three-year leases, lease purchase and contract hire are also available nationwide. For written details on the above or for any vehicle required please contact

Q11

HOLIDAY £

Austria 20.47
Belgium 60.80
France 9.74
Germany 2.9250
Greece 217
Holland 3.30
Ireland 1.0930
Italy 2120
Malta 0.5460
Portugal 226
Spain 199.75
Switzerland 2.4275
USA 1.60
Yugoslavia 1035

Q15

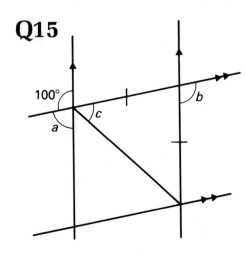

100°

a c b

Q8

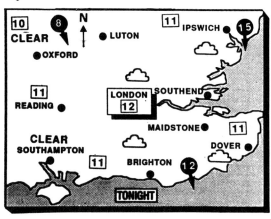

Well-known brands to clear

	Normally	Sale Price
Derwent 3-piece, 3-seater Suite inc FREE stool	£1,900	**£849.00**
Derwent Madison 3-seater Settee	£584.00	**£299.00**
Stonehill Wall Unit, Table and 4 Chairs	£899.00	**£599.00**
Charnwood 3-seater 3-piece Suite, choice of covers	£999.00	**£799.00**
Wm Barrett Lima 3-seater 3-piece Suite	£799.00	**£599.00**
Cintique Fireside Chair	£229.00	**£115.00**
Bunk Beds complete with mattresses	£199.00	**£129.00**
Stonehill 3-drawer Bureau Unit	£139.00	**£79.50**

Q9

874248

Q10

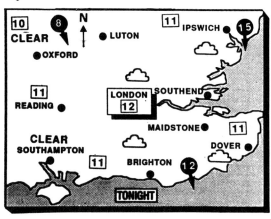

Q11

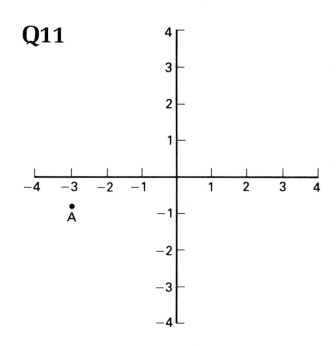

Q12

Q13

Tide Times
British Summer Time
July

	am	m	pm	m
Thurs 23	05.58	11.0	18.21	11.3
Fri 24	06.50	11.4	19.09	11.7
Sat 25	07.35	11.7	19.49	11.9
Sun 26	08.15	11.8	20.24	12.0
Mon 27	08.47	11.8	20.57	12.0
Tues 28	09.18	11.9	21.26	12.1
Wed 29	09.47	11.9	21.57	12.2

Q15

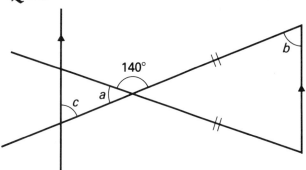

Q14

PLUS **20% OFF** REST OF SHARPS RANGE

Book 5 ● Test 14

Q8

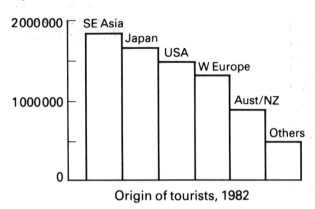

Origin of tourists, 1982

Q9

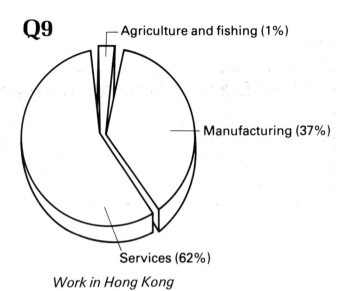

- Agriculture and fishing (1%)
- Manufacturing (37%)
- Services (62%)

Work in Hong Kong

Q10

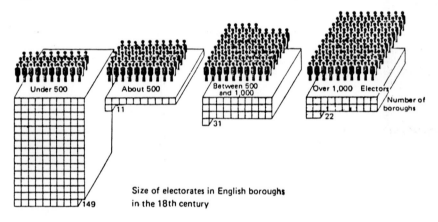

Under 500

About 500

Between 500 and 1,000

Over 1,000 Electors

Number of boroughs

11

31

22

149

Size of electorates in English boroughs in the 18th century

Q11

The ULTIMATE SOURCE

● WINTER SERVICE OFFER ●

BMW SERVICE KITS

BMW Carb Service Kits £6.90
BMW Twins (with round filter) £21.00
BMW Twins (with flat air filter) £23.00
With Oil Cooler Add £3.00
BMW K75 .... £26.00
BMW K100 .... £27.00
Service Kits include Air, Oil and Fuel Filters, Rocker Cover Gaskets, Plugs and Points where applicable.
Carb kits include Diaphragm. Gaskets and all 0 rings.

Q12

1981 Moto Guzzi Le Mans II 950cc
conversion. Superb condition. 26949
miles onlv. Red £2999

Q13

Of the 85,000 people who earn a living directly from timber in British Columbia, a tenth are employed along the Fraser.

Q14

In 1959 there were about 120,000 monks in Tibet—fully a quarter of all males.

Q15

Clothing Price List — from Oct 1984	Price+	p&p
Key Equipment 100% W'proof Nylon	£	£
Unlined one piece oversuit	27.50	1.50
Lined one piece suit	36.00	2.00
Lined two piece suit	45.00	2.00
Lined jacket only	28.00	1.50
Lined trousers only	17.00	1.50
Key Equipment Accessories		
Unlined o'mitts — waterproof nylon	2.50	30p
Balaclava underhelmet — acrylic	2.50	30p
Bodywarmer waistcoat, extra warm	7.50	1.00
Sea-Boot socks	2.95	50p
Reflective Safety Belt	3.50	30p
Goggles: Traditional Split Lens	17.25	30p

Aural Tests in Mathematics · John Murray

Q8

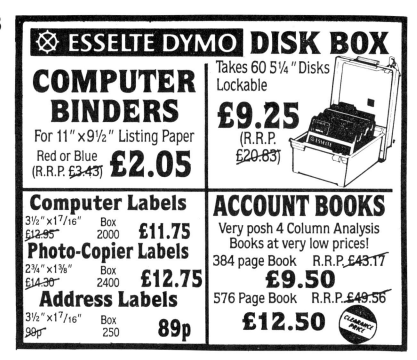

Q9

Q10

WESTON TO WELLS							
WESTON-super-Mare, Marine Parade	1415	1615	1815	2015	2215	2300
LOCKING ROAD, The Heron	1425	1625	1825	2025	2225	2310
LOCKING, Meadow Drive	1430	1630	1830	2030	2230	2315
BANWELL, School	1435	1635	1835	2035	2235	2320
SANDFORD, Church	1439	1639	1839	2039	2239	2324
WINSCOMBE, Browns Corner	1444	1644	1844	2044	2244	2329
CROSS, Manor Farm	1449	1649	1849	2049	2249	—
AXBRIDGE, Square	1453	1653	1853	2053	2253	—
CHEDDAR, Tweentown	1458	1658	1858	2058	2258	—
DRAYCOTT, Red Lion	1503	1703	1903	2103	2303	—
WESTBURY – Sub Mendip P.O.	1507	1707	1907	2107	2307	—
WELLS, Princes Road Bus Pk.	1517	1717	1917	2117	2317	—

continued ▶

Q11

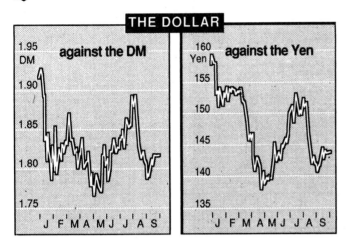

Q12

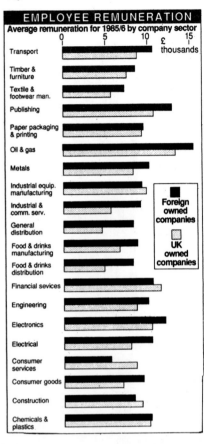

Q13

```
         SUPER—U
        FOUESNANT
       VOUS REMERCIE


   3218930288000
LAIT FRAIS L       4.30
0208 APERITIF     11.20
   1630
PYRENNEES OR       5.90
   2
CONSIGNE LIT        .75
   1630
PYRENNEES OR       5.90
   2
CONSIGNE LIT        .75
0400 FRUI/LEG      3.75
     S—T          32.55

   ART. 7
   TTL            32.55
   ESPECE        100.00
   RENDU          67.45

CAISS: 109      2126005
8427 18:08      22/08/87
```

Q14

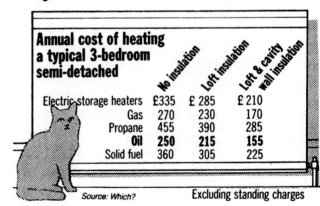

Annual cost of heating a typical 3-bedroom semi-detached	No insulation	Loft insulation	Loft & cavity wall insulation
Electric storage heaters	£335	£285	£210
Gas	270	230	170
Propane	455	390	285
Oil	**250**	**215**	**155**
Solid fuel	360	305	225

Source: Which?   Excluding standing charges

Q15

FIVE STAR ACCOUNT		
£25,000+	★	8.00% NET P.A
£10,000+	★	7.75% NET P A
£5,000+	★	7.50% NET P A
£2,000+	★	7.00% NET P A
£500+	★	6.75% NET P A

Q8

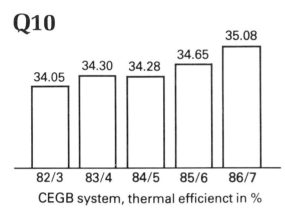

FLOTEX
Satin repelling Flotex. The perfect carpet for the kitchen. Sensational value.
Normally £13.50 sq.yd.

£12.50 SQ.YD.

CORMAR 'MIDAS TOUCH'
12' wide. Superb cut & loop carpet in 7 colours.
Made in UK.
Normally £6.50 sq.yd.

£5.99 SQ.YD.

HERITAGE 'DONNA'
12' wide. Attractive twist pile textured to grace any home. 7 colourways. Made in UK.
Normally £6.75 sq.yd.

£6.25 SQ.YD.

Q9

BRITISH MADE ECONOMY RADIALS

60 % OFF *

PLUS EXTRA 10% DISCOUNT
FOR THE FIRST 20 CUSTOMERS EACH DAY!

Q10

82/3	83/4	84/5	85/6	86/7
34.05	34.30	34.28	34.65	35.08

CEGB system, thermal efficienct in %

Q11

★ **SPECIAL OFFER** ★

Class 3 HGV 5-day courses - **£265** + **test**
for August & September only

Q12

TYSON		TUCKER
June 30, 1966	Birthday	Dec. 28, 1958
21	Age	28
Brooklyn, New York	Birthplace	Grand Rapids, Michigan
15st 10lb (approx)	Weight	16st 2lb (approx)
5ft 11½in	Height	6ft 5in
71in	Reach	81½in
43in	Chest (norm)	42in
45in	Chest (exp)	45½in
16in	Bicep	16½in
14in	Forearm	13½in
34in	Waist	34in
27in	Thigh	22½in
18ins	Calf	16½in
11in	Ankle	10in
19¾in	Neck	17½in
8in	Wrist	8in
13in	Fist	13¼in

Q13

YOU CAN SEE FROM THIS "READY RECKONER" THAT YOU CAN PROTECT YOUR FAMILY FOR UP TO £130,000 FROM JUST PENNIES PER DAY

	PLAN A	PLAN B	PLAN C	PLAN D	PLAN E
AMOUNT PAYABLE ON DEATH	£10,000	£20,000	£35,000	£50,000	£65,000
TOTAL COVER IF DEATH ACCIDENTAL	£20,000	£40,000	£70,000	£100,000	£130,000
AGE NEAREST BIRTHDAY	AMOUNT YOU PAY MONTHLY				
20-30	£5.00	£6.00	£7.35	£10.50	£13.65
31-35	£5.00	£6.20	£9.10	£13.00	£16.90
36-40	£5.40	£8.40	£12.95	£18.50	£24.05
41-45	£6.00	£12.00	£19.25	£27.50	—
46-50	£9.30	£18.60	£30.80	—	—
51-55	£14.70	£29.40	—	—	—

Q14

MR KIPLING CAKES

Six Almond Slices

NO ARTIFICIAL COLOURS OR FLAVOURS

~~69p~~
59p
Pack of 6

Q15

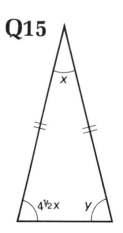

x

$4½x$ y

Aural Tests in Mathematics · John Murray

Q8

SALE PRICE **£249.95**
NO DEPOSIT INSTANT CREDIT.
ONLY £11 MONTHLY.

Q9

SCOTTISH—Div 2

Albion	(1)..1	Alloa	(0)..0
Arbroath	(1)..3	Berwick	(0)..1
Ayr	(2)..4	Queen's Pk	(1)..1
E Stirling	(0)..0	St Johnstone	(0)..2
Montrose	(0)..1	Stenhousemuir	(0)..0
Stirling	(1)..2	Cowdenbeath	(0)..0
Stranraer	(0)..1	Brechin	(0)..1

Q10

Cantonese   Siyi   Chaozhou   Others

Chinese groups in Hong Kong

Q11

BAHAMAS

Florida
Grand Bahama
Freeport
Miami
Great Abaco
Nassau
Eleuthera
New Providence
Andros
Cat Is.
Great Exuma
San Salvador
Long Is.
Acklins Is.

0   200
km

Great Inagua

Q12

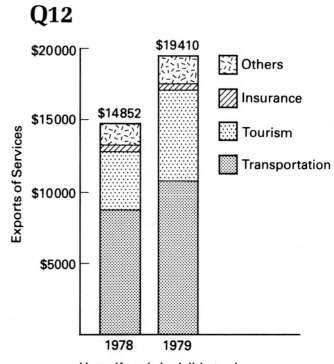

Hong Kong's invisible trade

continued ▶

Q13

DATE	DESTINATION	NO. OF NIGHTS	ACCOMMODATION		DEPARTURE AIRPORT	PRICE	FLIGHT ONLY
29 SEPT	C. DORADA/AZAHAR	7	APARTMENT	AO	GATWICK	£139	£69
29 SEPT	MAJORCA	7	APARTMENT	AO	GATWICK	£119	£99
30 SEPT	COSTA BLANCA	7	APARTMENT	AO	LUTON	£145	£69
30 SEPT	RHODES	14	1 CROWN	BB	BRISTOL	£279	£119
30 SEPT	TENERIFE	14	4 CROWN	HB	GATWICK	£249	£119
4 OCT	IBIZA	14	APARTMENT	AO	GATWICK	£245	£119
5 OCT	C. BRAVA/DORADA	7	APARTMENT	AO	GATWICK	£147	£99
8 OCT	ALGARVE	7	APARTMENT	AO	LUTON	£278	£109
9 OCT	NEAPOLITAN RIV.	14	2 CROWN	HB	GATWICK	£340	£99
15 OCT	SICILY (CATANIA)	7	2 CROWN	BB	GATWICK	£249	£119

SEE YOUR TRAVEL AGENT NOW!

Q14

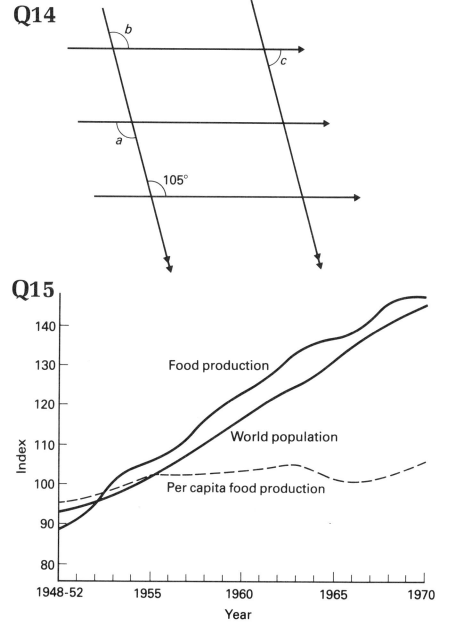

Q15

World population and food production

Q8

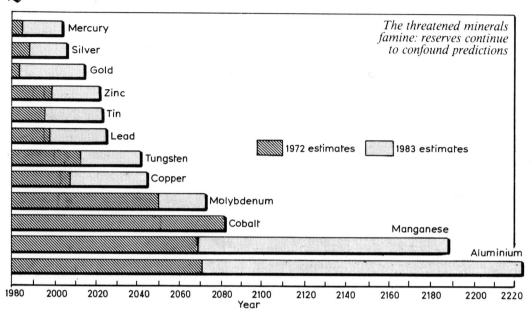

The threatened minerals famine: reserves continue to confound predictions

Mercury, Silver, Gold, Zinc, Tin, Lead, Tungsten, Copper, Molybdenum, Cobalt, Manganese, Aluminium

1972 estimates | 1983 estimates

Year: 1980, 2000, 2020, 2040, 2060, 2080, 2100, 2120, 2140, 2160, 2180, 2200, 2220

Q9

VOLVO

IN WATFORD

1987 (D) 740 GLE auto saloon, silver metallic, black leather, all options ..£12,995

1987 (D) 340 GLE limited edition, many extras £7,495

1986 (D) 340 GL auto, 5-door £6,195

1986 (C) 340 GL 3-door hatchback, ocean blue metallic £5,195

1985 (B) 760 GLE saloon, metallic silver, 1 owner, excellent throughout £9,995

1984 (B) '85 model 760 GLE, graphite, low mileage, superb throughout £10,495

1984 (A) 240 DL manual estate, 1 owner, excellent throughout £5,695

1987 demonstration models available

Please phone for further details

Q10

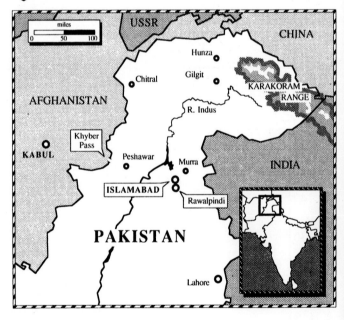

Q11

Table three — Recommendations by authorities	
Recommended microcomputer	**Number of authorities**
None	2
RML 380-Z	53
Apple II	8
Commodore Pet	26
Sharp MZ-80K	1
Tandy TRS-80	2
Acorn Atom	3
BBC	35
Sinclair ZX-80/81	2
Other	4

continued ▶

Q12

60/50 SERIES HIGH PERFORMANCE	
	From
185/60HR×13	£29.90
205/60HR×13	£42.00
205/60VR×13	£46.00
185/60HR×14	£35.60
195/60HR×14	£38.30
195/60VR×14	£55.00
195/60HR×15	£37.50
195/50VR×15	£61.75
205/55VR×16	£100.00
225/50VR×16	£100.00

Q13

BED SALE

FREE Velour Headboard with all Beds over £80

SINGLE DIVAN	**£39.99**
DOUBLE DIVAN	**£79.99**
PINE BUNK BEDS Only	**£89.99**
Antique PINE DOUBLE BED	**£129.99**
SAVOY 4ft. 6in. Four Jumbo Drawers	**£159**

★ Credit facilities available

Q14

TYPICAL EXAMPLE - PANDA 750L	
Cash Price (inc. est. on the road costs)	£4,144.70†
Deposit (35% minimum)	£1,450.65
Balance to be financed	£2,694.05
Interest charges (APR 6.41%)	£266.59
Total debt	£2,960.64
Total debt of £2,960.64 payable by 36 monthly instalments of	£82.24
Weekly equivalent*	£18.98
Total credit price	£4,411.29

Q15

MILLIONS OF

REFUSE SACKS

MUST GO DUE TO WAREHOUSE CLEARANCE!

ALL PRICES INCLUDE V.A.T.

ATTENTION!

FIRMS, SHOPS, RESTAURANTS, FACTORIES, HOUSEWIVES

SAVE £ £ £'s!

BLACK REFUSE SACKS — As used by Govt. depots. Size 25in x 39in: 200 — £10.95, 400 — £20.65, 1,000 — £45.00.

ALUMINIUM FOIL — 148ft. long in 18in dispenser £3.95 or 3 for £11.50.

SWING BINLINERS — Size 23in x 28in: 300 — £6.95.

CLINGFILM — 1,000ft approx roll in 13in dispenser — £3.95 or 3 for £11.50.

PEDAL BIN LINERS — Size 17in x 17in: 300 — £3.95.

WATERPROOF, LIGHTWEIGHT

STRONG TARPAULINS

LARGE SIZE 18ft x 12ft ONLY £10.95   GIANT SIZE 23ft x 18ft ONLY £16.95

Q8

■ MORE than three million investors have told BP they are interested in buying shares when the Government sells off its stake in the oil giant soon. Enquiries about the share offer are now flooding in at 150,000 a day.

Q9

The two front mats each measure 25½" long and 19½" wide and those for the back are each 13" long and 19½" wide

Q10

◄ Only with a food processor can you shred, slice, chip, mix, blend and purée so easily. And only when you order a Tefal Foodmaster from us, will you receive absolutely FREE 8 pieces of Tefal non-stick Homebake comprising: 2 sandwich tins. Swiss roll tin, 12 hole bun tin and 4 tartlet tins.

Recommended price £26

Q11

For a minimum investment of £10,000 you can earn 8.05% net, paid annually (11.03%* gross). And for £25,000 or more, you can earn 8.20% net, paid annually (11.23%* gross).

Q12

SCENTED POLYANTHUS
Originally grown in peat pots, lovely range of warm rich colours - perennial in habit for sun or part shade. 10 for £4.95; 20 for £7.95; 50 for £16.30; 100 for £31.00 carr paid.

Q13

Thompson Holidays offer seven nights in Rome from £341 (sharing double twin room) now—or £313 in October.
They also offer a four-night Rome "seasonal saver" from £225 per person until October 23. Four nights in Vienna costs from £278.

Q14

INDIA/NEPAL
North India £465 24 days
South India £460 24 days
White Water Racing
            £275 10 days
Trekking   £350 10 days

Q15

Smith looked a favourite for the sack when QPR lost four of the last five matches last season. They scored just four goals and conceded 18.

Q8

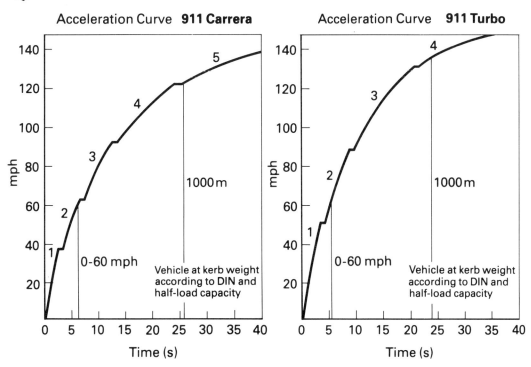

Q9

TOURING & CAMPING CHARGES per night		
Children under 3 years – FREE		
Children after 15th birthday – ADULT RATE		
ALL CHARGES INCLUDE V.A.T AT 15%		
		Daily Rates
before May 23rd	Adults	£1.40
	Children	FREE
May 23rd–June 27th	Adults	£1.80
	Children	FREE
June 28th–July 11th	Adults	£1.80
	Children	90p
July 12th–July 18th	Adults	£1.90
	Children	95p
July 19th–July 25th	Adults	£2.20
	Children	£1.10
July 26th–August 8th	Adults	£2.30
	Children	£1.15
August 9th–August 15th	Adults	£2.20
	Children	£1.10
August 16th–August 22nd	Adults	£2.10
	Children	£1.05
August 23rd–August 29th	Adults	£1.80
	Children	90p
August 30th–September 5th	Adults	£1.80
	Children	FREE
September 6th onwards	Adults	£1.40
	Children	FREE

EXTRA – Electricity hook-up facility (inclusive of V.A.T.)
£1.00 (6 amp) – £1.15 (10 amp & 16 amp per night

Q10

continued

Q11

COME AND SEE FOR YOURSELVES
THE THOUSANDS OF ITEMS WE HAVE TO
CLEAR FROM TOP QUALITY MAIL ORDER
FIRMS ....

MENS WEAR

	Catalogue Price	Our Price
Active Tops	£11.99	**£4.99**
Swimming Trunks	£8.99	**£2.50**
Cords and Jeans	£17.99	**£8.99**
Adidas Socks		Only **£1.99**
Linen Type Jackets		Only **£4.99**
Propeller Aircrew Shirts	£9.99	**£4.99**
Cotton Sweaters		Only **£3.99**
Check Shirts	£7.99	**£2.99**
Slazenger Slipovers	£8.99	**£4.50**
Good Assortment of Trousers		from **£4.99**

MISCELLANEOUS STOCKS of Childrens Wear, Handbags, Corsetry, Bras, Bedding, Curtains etc. etc.

LADIES BLOUSES - Large stock to choose from, big assortment of sizes and colours from only **£1.99** each

LATEST SCOOP - CHILDRENS TEE-SHIRTS Only **99p** Each

LADIES WEAR

	Catalogue Price	Our Price
Cotton Dresses	£11.99	**£5.99**
Berkertex Dresses	£25.99	**£9.99**
2pc Suits by 'Peepers'	£42.99	**£14.99**
Track Suits	£20.99	**£8.99**
Vee Neck Jumpers	£4.99	**£1.99**
Smart Flying Suits	£20.99	**£8.99**
Tee Shirts	£4.99	**£1.50**
Summer Weight Anoraks	£22.99	**£6.99**
Special Buy - Jackets	£29.99	**£4.99**
Polycotton Tops	£4.99	**£1.99**
Negligee Sets	£12.99	**£6.50**
Summer Dressing Gowns	£9.99	**£4.99**
Slacks, fair selection		from **£2.99**
Full length Slips		Now **£1.99**
Super Cotton Skirts		Only **£2.99**
Towel Look Shorts		now only **25p pr**

Fantastic Selection of Bra's - famous makes such as Berlei, Gossard, Playtex, Triumph, Naturana, etc. from **£1.99** each

Q12

% DISCOUNT OFF RETAIL GUIDELINE PRICE

G-Plan, Nathan, Meredew, Stateroom
Discontinued Models

WELL KNOWN BRANDS TO CLEAR

	Normally	Sale Price
Derwent 3 Pce Suite incl. Free Stool	£1900.00	**£849.00**
Relyon Sofa Bed	£169.00	**£129.00**
Derwent Madison 3 Seater Settee	£584.00	**£299.00**
Stonehill Wall Unit, Table & 4 Chairs	£899.00	**£599.00**
Charnwood 3 Str 3 Pce Suite, choice of colours	£999.00	**£799.00**
Wm Barrett Lima 3 Seater 3 Piece Suite	£799.00	**£599.00**
Cintique Fireside Chair	£229.00	**£115.00**
Bunk Beds complete with Mattresses	£199.00	**£129.00**
Stonehill 3 Drawer Bureau Unit	£139.00	**£79.50**

G PLAN Main Stockist
NO ONE BEATS OUR PRICES
Access & Barclaycard welcome
FREE DELIVERY
Monday-Saturday 9am-5.30pm
Half-Day Closing Wednesday 1pm

IDEAL HOMES
Queen's Road, Clevedon
Tel: 872186

Q13

PRINGLES GARDEN SUPPLIES

Peat, 80 litre — **£2.00**
Peat, small — **80p**
Grow-bags, large — **£1.25**
Seed/Potting, 40 ltr — **£2.30**
Cornish Grit, per bag — **£1.00**
Bristol Grit, bag — **80p**
Vermiculite

Mendip Top Soil - 10 bags - **£9.00**
Sedge Top Soil - 10 bags - **£8.00**
Mushroom Comp. - 10 bags - **£6.00**
Organic Fertilizer, 40 litre - **£3.75**
Silver Sand (coarse), bag - **£1.00**
Horse Manure - **60p**
Potatoes, Gro-more

PATIO SLABS, BAGGED & SEALED AGGREGATES

2 x 2 Grey **£1.50**
2 x 1'6" **£1.25**
2 x 1 .... **90p**
18 x 18 .... **£1.00**
1 x 1 .... **75p**
York 18 x 18 Grey **£1.25**

L/stone Chipping, clean... **80p**
Blended **80p**
Limestone Dust **80p**
Morton Sand **85p**
Holm Sand **80p**
Cement **£3.75**
Scalping **80p**
Driveway Chippings
Charstock, per bag - **£1.00**
Pea Gravel, per bag - **£1.10**

Patios Laid, Concret Blocks
(Colours extra to order)
Stone Flower Pots, Ornamental Planters, Garden Edging and Bird Baths

FREE DELIVERY, C.O.D.

Pringles Farm, Chepstow 77165

Q14

Uprate your car's suspension. Fit
CENTURION SUPREME
High performance, Gas-filled
SHOCK ABSORBERS
FITTED WHILE-YOU-WAIT

eg To fit CORTINA 3/4, ALPINE, CAVALIER Mk I, ESCORT Mk II.

EACH FROM ONLY £17·30 + £2.60 VAT

OR PAIR FITTED FROM ONLY £31·30 + £4.70 VAT

GUARANTEED FOR AS LONG AS YOU OWN THE CAR THEY ARE FITTED TO.

Q15

WOODSPRING FENCING

Hardworth Estate, Lincoln
Tel: Lincoln 55510

Top quality lap panel treated with golden barrettine timber guard

Price Per Panel		Posts	
6 x 6	**£8.50**	8ft	**£3.25**
6 x 5	**£7.65**	7ft	**£3.00**
6 x 4	**£6.75**	6ft	**£2.75**
6 x 3	**£5.95**	5ft	**£2.50**

Trellis panels, gates made to size
Stockist of met. posts, sand, chippings and cement.

Also top quality shiplap sheds, all sizes

Free Estimates for Fence Erection

PATIO SLABS
18" x 18" - **£1.35**

Open 7 days a week 8am - 5pm

Prices include VAT

Q8

2 COURSE MEAL £5.95

● Children are always welcome
  – under 13's £3.95p
  – under 5's eat FREE*

★ (one child per adult)

Today!

Q9

```
LAWN  SEED
500 gm    £1.70
 2 kg    £6.50
10 kg   £32.00
```

Q10

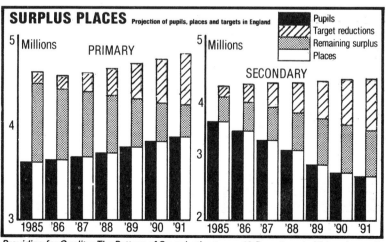

SURPLUS PLACES Projection of pupils, places and targets in England

- Pupils
- Target reductions
- Remaining surplus
- Places

PRIMARY

SECONDARY

Providing for Quality: The Pattern of Organization to age 19. Department of Education and Science.

continued

Aural Tests in Mathematics · John Murray

Q11

WEATHER ABROAD

(Midday: c, cloud; d, drizzle; f, fair;
fg, fog; r, rain; s, sun; sn, snow)

		Max C	F
Akrotiri	s	21	70
Amsterdam	c	12	54
Barcelona	f	17	63
Biarritz	c	12	54
Cologne	f	13	55
Copenhagen	s	13	55
Corfu	fg	21	70
Dublin	c	11	52
Dubrovnik	c	8	46
Florence	c	14	57
Gibraltar	s	20	68
Innsbruck	fg	12	54
Lisbon	s	18	64
Madrid	s	15	59
Majorca	f	16	61
Malta	s	16	61
Milan	f	12	54
Moscow	c	23	73
Munich	c	7	45
Naples	fg	16	61
Nice	f	16	61
Paris	f	12	54
Rhodes	s	23	73
Rome	f	14	57
Stockholm	s	12	54
Tangier	s	22	72
Tenerife	s	20	68
Venice	f	15	59
Vienna	c	14	57

Q12

MODEL	MRP	FLEET PRICE
BLUEBIRD		
1.6 LX, 4 door	£7,790	£6,783
1.6 LX, 5 door	£8,015	£6,979
1.8 LX, 4 door	£8,090	£7,044
1.8 LX, 5 door	£8,315	£7,241
1.8 SLX, 4 door	£8,948	£7,792
1.8 SLX, 5 door	£9,174	£7,988
2.0 SLX, 4 door	£9,199	£8,010
2.0 SLX, 5 door	£9,425	£8,207
2.0 SGX, 4 door	£11,000	£9,579
2.0 SGX, 5 door	£11,224	£9,774
2.0 LX Diesel, 4 door	£8,425	£7,336
2.0 LX Diesel, 5 door	£8,649	£7,531
1.8 ZX Turbo, 4 door	£11,224	£9,774
1.8 ZX Turbo, 5 door	£11,450	£9,970
2.0 DX Estate	£8,395	£7,310
2.0 GL Estate	£9,195	£8,007

**Choice of models. 4 or 5 door
Diesel, Turbo, 1.6/1.8/2.0**

Aural Tests in Mathematics · John Murray

Q13

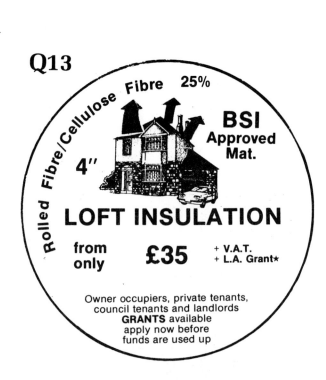

Rolled Fibre/Cellulose Fibre 25%

BSI Approved Mat.

4″

LOFT INSULATION

from only **£35** + V.A.T. + L.A. Grant★

Owner occupiers, private tenants,
council tenants and landlords
GRANTS available
apply now before
funds are used up

Q14

**Breakdown of support for parties'
education policies**

	Jan %	Feb %	March %	April %
Con	25	30	25	28
Lab	40	35	34	32
All	13	16	19	19
Don't know	22	19	21	20

Q15

	Originally	NOW
Vi Spring. Pair of 3′3″ divans	£2,077.50	**£1,495**
Relyon Braemar 4′6″ wide divan set	£799	**£679**
Sleepeezee Backmaster 4′6″ wide divan set	£549.95	**£469.95**
Sleepeezee. 3′ wide twosome storage bed	£575	**£449**

Q8

Q9

Q10

Your Plan Selection Chart
Which level of cover would you like?

Age now		£15.00 per month		£12.50 per month		£10.00 per month		£7.50 per month	
MALE	FEMALE	Non-smoker	Standard	Non-smoker	Standard	Non-smoker	Standard	Non-smoker	Standard
18-29	18-33	£144,315	£92,657	£118,788	£76,267	£89,309	£59,878	£64,863	£43,488
30	34	141,805	90,597	116,722	74,573	87,820	58,547	63,782	42,521
31	35	134,773	85,829	110,934	70,648	83,639	55,466	60,745	40,283
32	36	124,485	79,939	102,466	65,799	77,489	51,659	56,278	37,519
33	37	115,656	74,125	91,939	61,014	72,181	47,902	52,424	34,790
34	38	105,211	67,948	83,894	55,929	65,865	43,910	47,837	31,891
35	39	93,722	62,721	77,144	51,627	60,566	40,533	43,988	29,438
36	40	84,935	56,624	69,912	46,608	54,888	36,592	39,864	26,576
37	41	77,656	51,935	63,919	42,749	50,183	33,562	36,447	24,375
38	42	70,291	46,860	57,858	38,572	45,424	30,283	32,991	21,994
39	43	62,721	41,815	51,627	34,418	40,533	27,022	29,438	19,625
40	44	56,232	37,575	46,286	30,929	36,340	24,282	26,393	17,636
41	45	50,962	33,974	41,947	27,965	32,933	21,955	23,918	15,945
42	46	45,551	30,424	37,495	25,043	29,437	19,661	21,379	14,280
43	47	40,973	27,361	33,726	22,522	26,479	17,682	19,231	12,842
44	48	36,728	24,486	30,232	20,155	23,735	15,824	17,238	11,492
45	49	33,010	22,037	27,172	18,139	21,333	14,241	15,494	10,343
46	50	29,868	19,887	24,584	16,370	19,301	12,852	14,018	9,334
47	51	26,909	17,960	22,150	14,783	17,390	11,606	12,630	8,429
48	52	24,339	16,210	20,034	13,343	15,729	10,476	11,424	—
49	53	21,859	14,586	17,993	12,006	14,127	9,426	10,260	—
50	54	19,742	13,172	16,251	10,843	12,758	8,512	9,266	—
51	—	17,841	11,885	14,686	9,784	11,530	7,681	8,374	—
52	—	16,081	10,727	13,238	8,831	10,393	—	—	—
53	—	14,533	9,684	11,964	7,971	9,393	—	—	—
54	—	13,172	8,777	10,843	7,224	8,512	—	—	—

This is not a savings plan and it therefore acquires no surrender or cash value. Premiums are used to provide the maximum sum possible should death occur during the period of the policy.

Q11

Q12

Tide times
British Summer Time April

	am	m	pm	m
Thurs (9)	04.03	9.0	16.44	9.4
Fri (10)	05.05	10.0	17.34	10.4
Sat (11)	05.50	11.0	18.17	11.4
Sun (12)	06.31	11.9	18.56	12.1
Mon (13)	07.10	12.6	19.35	12.7
Tues (14)	07.49	13.1	20.12	13.1
Wed (15)	08.27	13.4	20.48	13.3

Q13

Q14

Q15

Q8

OPENING HOURS MONDAY TO FRIDAY

9·30 AM until 5pm. ~~3·30~~ PM

🏢 **THE CO-OPERATIVE BANK**

We've got more time for you

Q9

Q10

Q11

Country	18 to 24-year-old conservation volunteers (1) %	Unemployment %
Brazil	19	3.4 to 29 (2)
Philippines	13	25
Yugoslavia	12	15
West Germany	7	10
Switzerland	6	0.7
UK	5	11.7
France	5	11.5
USA	4	6.3
Sweden	3	2.9
Japan	1	2.7

(1) MORI
(2) Sources: low figure (Brazilian Embassy), high (EEC).

Q12

Q15

Q14

Q13

Q8

Spear and Jackson 22" Handsaw

16oz Steel Shaft Claw Hammer

3.5 metre Aluminium Extension Ladder, extends to 6.5 metres.

Pack of 4 White Chubb Locks for wooden casement windows, including key.

Q9

WOODSPRING FENCING

Hardworth Estate, Lincoln
Tel: Lincoln 55510

Top quality lap panel treated with golden barrettine timber guard

Price Per Panel	Posts
6 x 6 - £8.50	8ft - £3.25
6 x 5 - £7.65	7ft - £3.00
6 x 4 - £6.75	6ft - £2.75
6 x 3 - £5.95	5ft - £2.50

Trellis panels, gates made to size
Stockist of met. posts, sand, chippings and cement.

Also top quality shiplap sheds, all sizes

Free Estimates for Fence Erection

PATIO SLABS
18" x 18" - £1.35

Open
7 days a week
8am - 5pm
Prices include VAT

Q10

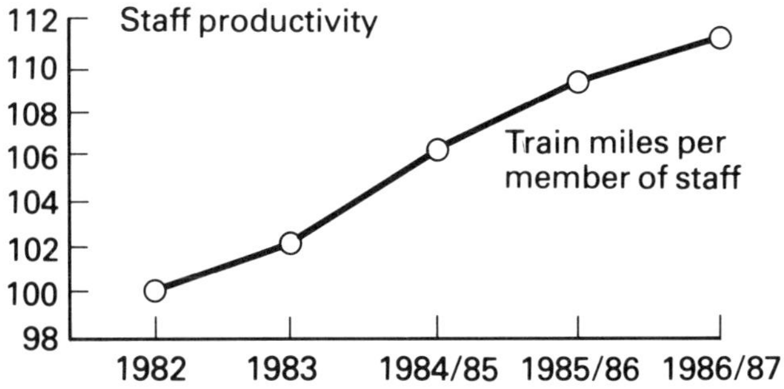

Q11

BRISTOL ROVERS FOOTBALL CLUB PLC

SEASON TICKETS 1987-1988

LAST CHANCE

BOOK BEFORE JULY 17 AND SAVE

	BEFORE JULY 17	AFTER JULY 17
STAND SEATS		
ADULT	£99.00	£110.00
JUV/OAP	£65.00	£75.00
FAMILY (3)	£190.00	£220.00
FAMILY (4)	£245.00	£285.00
STANDING		
ADULT	£47.00	£52.00
JUV/OAP	£22.50	£25.00
UNDER-11s	£12.00	£14.00
FAMILY (3)	£100.00	£110.00
FAMILY (4)	£120.00	£135.00

TEL. 510363/510828 or post or call in at: 468 Stapleton Road, Eastville, Bristol Mon.-Fri. 10 a.m.-4 p.m.

Q12

EXAMPLES OF REPAYMENTS AT 18.86% APR VARIABLE

Amount of Loan £	36 MONTHS		60 MONTHS		90 MONTHS		120 MONTHS	
	Monthly Repayment £	Total Repayment £	Monthly Repayment £	Total Repayment £	Monthly Repayment £	Total Repayment £	Monthly Repayment £	Total Repayment £
1000	35.85	1290.60	25.07	1504.20	19.96	1796.40	–	–
3000	107.56	3872.16	75.20	4512.00	59.89	5390.10	52.90	6348.00
4000	143.41	5162.76	100.27	6016.20	79.86	7187.40	70.54	8464.80
5000	179.26	6453.36	125.34	7520.40	99.82	8983.80	88.17	10580.40
7500	268.89	9680.04	188.01	11280.60	149.74	13476.60	132.26	15871.20

Q13

TIDE TABLE

Week starting July 17th

	am	mtrs	pm	mtrs
Fri	–	–	12.20	10.7
Sat	12.45	10.7	1.06	10.2
Sun	1.35	10.2	1.59	9.7
Mon ...	2.34	9.7	3.00	9.4
Tue	3.42	9.5	4.13	9.4
Wed ...	4.56	9.6	5.24	9.8
Thur ...	5.57	9.9	6.19	10.2
Fri	6.47	10.3	7.05	10.6

Q14

FRESH FISH

For your freezer - direct from Brixham Trawlers.

EVERY SUNDAY MORNING 9.30am-12.30pm.
Much fresher! Much cheaper! Much more variety!

5lb Plaice Fillet £7.15	5lb Herring £3.00
5lb Cod Fillet (fresh) £6.45	5lb Smoked Haddock £6.95
5lb Coley Fillet £4.25	5lb Smoked Cod ... £6.50
5lb Cod Fillet (frozen) £5.95	5lb Golden Cutlets . £5.50
5lb Haddock Fillet .. £6.95	5lb Smoked Mackerel £4.00
5lb Mackerel £2.50	5lb Kippers £4.20
5lb Dabs £1.50	5lb Hake ..... As available
5lb Plaice, from £2.50	5lb Rainbow Trout .. £5.95
5lb Lemon Sole(s) .. £4.50	Prawns in shell £2.60 per lb
5lb Lemon Sole(l) .. £7.00	Prawns peeled £4.45 per lb
5lb Whiting £1.50	Cockles ...... £1.60 per lb

All above - whole fish, cleaned & gutted.
PLUS! PLUS! PLUS! Bream, Bass, Coley, Conger, Gurnets, Monk, Plaice, Fillet, Pollock, Rock-Salmon, Squid, Salmon, Sprats. All fish available by the pound.
All fish and prices subject to market fluctuation.

Q15

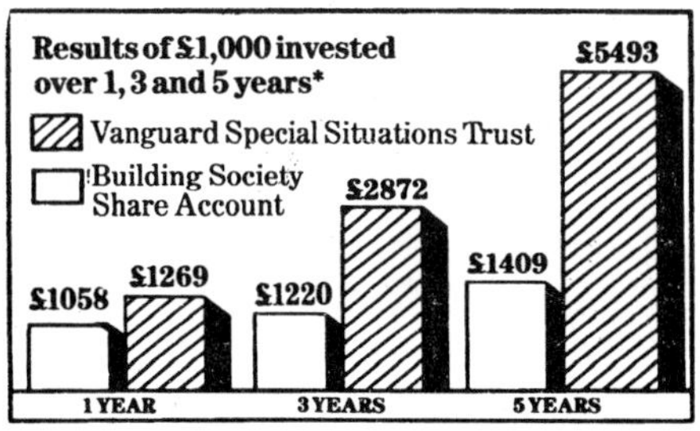

Q8

ACCOUNT	MINIMUM INVESTMENT	NOTICE ON WITHDRAWALS	INTEREST CREDITED/PAID	INTEREST PER ANNUM		
				NET (BASIC RATE TAX PAID)	CAR †	GROSS* CAR
No. 1 Income	£5,000	3 months	Monthly	8.00%	8.30%	11.37%
Special 3 month	£5,000	3 months	Annually 1st July	8.25%	8.25%	11.30%
Bristol Triple Bonus	£25,000	7 days/None	Annually 1st June	8.10%	8.10%	11.10%
	£10,000	7 days/None		7.80%	7.80%	10.68%
	£5,000	7 days		7.55%	7.55%	10.34%
	£500	7 days		7.30%	7.30%	10.00%

Q9

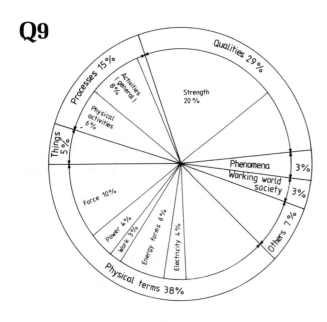

Qualities 29%
Processes 15%
Activities (general) 8%
Physical activities 6%
Things 5%
Strength 20%
Phenomena 3%
Working world society 3%
Others 7%
Force 10%
Power 4%
Work 3%
Energy forms 6%
Electricity 4%
Physical terms 38%

Q10

Aural Tests in Mathematics · John Murray

continued ▶

Q11

> **GLASGOW CARPET CENTRE**
>
> 17 The Centre, (next to Odeon)
> Carpets from £2.99 sq yd to
> £32.99 sq yd
> *Expertly fitted - Free estimates*
> Carpets - Vinyls - Rugs - Tiles - Accessories
> Roll ends usually available
> saving up to 50% off normal prices.

Q12

> ★ Patio Slabs - all patterns, shapes
>   & sizes
> ★ Cotswold Stone Flower Pots
> ★ Screen Wall Blocks
> ★ Copings
> ★ Path Edgings
> ★ Cotswold Stone Walling
> ★ Sand Chipping & Cement
>
> Also Lap Fencing, e.g. 6' x 6' - **£8.50**
>
> **Open 7 days a week
> 8.00am - 4.30pm**
> *Prices include VAT
> and prompt delivery service*
>
> **POWER CONCRETE
> PRODUCTS**
>
> Cash on Delivery
>
> Patio laying service - Free Estimates

Q13

> # clutches: as only
> # we know how.

FRONT-WHEEL-DRIVE	R.R.P.	OFFER
NOVA 1.2, 1.3	52.00	44.20
ASTRA 1.3	52.00	44.20
CAVALIER 1.6	53.00	45.05
REAR-WHEEL-DRIVE		
CHEVETTE	37.70	32.04
HC VIVA	37.70	32.04
CAVALIER 1.6	44.95	38.20

ALL PRICES PLUS V.A.T.

Q14

$$A = \begin{pmatrix} 1 & 2 \\ 0 & 2 \end{pmatrix}$$

$$B = \begin{pmatrix} -1 & 3 \\ 2 & 0 \end{pmatrix}$$

Q15

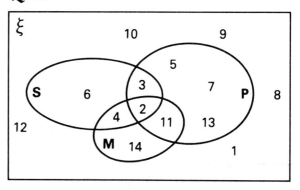

Book 5 ● Extension 1

Q8

Mondays to Saturdays

SAND BAY			0940	1040	1140	1240	1340	1440	1540	1640	1740	1840	...	..
Kewstoke, Toll Gate			0947	1047	1147	1247	1347	1447	1547	1647	1747	1847	...	..
Old Pier			0953	1053	1153	1253	1353	1453	1553	1653	1753	1853	...	..
BUS STATION (Bay 6) arr.		...	**1001**	**1101**	**1201**	**1301**	**1401**	**1501**	**1601**	**1701**	**1801**	**1901**	...	..
BUS STATION (Bay 6) dep.	**0905**		**1105**				**1405**		**1605**		**1805**			
Royal Hospital	0909		1109				1409		1609		1809			
Uphill, Post Office	0913		1113				1413		1613		1813			
Bleadon, Anchor Inn	0919		1119				1419		1619		1819			
Brean, Central Stores	0935		1135				1435		1635		1835			
Brean, Leisure Centre	0940		1140				1440		1640		1840			
Berrow, Triangle	0947		1147				1447		1647		1847			
Burnham-on-Sea, Sea View Road	0953		1153				1453		1653					
BURNHAM-ON-SEA, Pier Street	0955		1155				1455		1655		1855			
HIGHBRIDGE, Church	1003		1203				1503		1703					

HIGHBRIDGE, Church			1010		1210				1510		1710			
BURNHAM-ON-SEA, Pier Street			1020		1220				1520		1720	1900		
Burnham-on-Sea, Sea View Road			1022		1222				1522		1722	1902		
Berrow Triangle			1028		1228				1528		1728	1908		
Brean, Leisure Centre			1035		1235				1535		1735	1915		
Brean, Central Stores			1040		1240				1540		1740	1920		
Bleadon, Anchor Inn			1056		1256				1556		1756	1936		
Uphill, Post Office			1102		1302				1602		1802	1942		
Royal Hospital			1106		1306				1606		1806	1946		
BUS STATION (Bay 2)	**0910**	**1010**	**1110**	**1210**	**1310**	**1410**	**1510**	**1610**	**1710**	**1810**	**1950**		
Old Pier	0918	1018	1118	1218	1318	1418	1518	1618	1718	1818			
Kewstoke, Toll Gate	0924	1024	1124	1224	1324	1424	1524	1624	1724	1824			
SAND BAY	0931	1031	1131	1231	1331	1431	1531	1631	1731	1831			

Q9

Q10

Q11

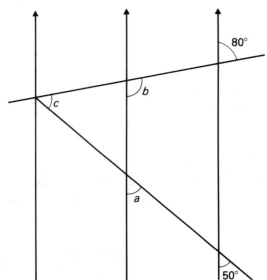

Q12

Q13

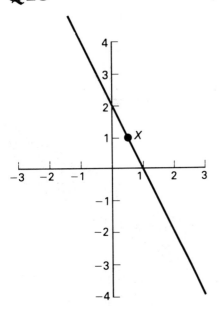

Q14

Q15

784350

Q8

SPENCERS
CARVERY
RESTAURANT

Catherines Inn
BLEADON
WESTON-SUPER-MARE

Real Ales

from a Farmhouse ploughmans lunch
to a 16oz Rump Steak at only **£5.95**

3 Course Family Restaurant
Adult **£5.95** and Children **£3.50**
Children under 3 **FREE**
Bookings available now!
Tel: Weston-super-Mare 812275
Come and join us!

Home Cooking

Q9

DIRECT FROM THE MANUFACTURER
PATIO SLABS
TOP QUALITY IN 5 COLOURS

Riven	Cobblestone and
18"x 18" £1.35	Rustic Brick
2'x 2' £1.95	18"x 18" £1.45

* Patio Slabs— all patterns, shapes and sizes
* Cotswold Stone flower pots
* Screen wall blocks
* Copings
* Path edgings
* Cotswold Stone walling
* Sand chipping and cement

ALSO LAP FENCING
eg 6ft x 6ft **£8.50**
PRICES INC VAT
MINIMUM ORDER OF 30

**PATIO
LAYING
SERVICE**
FREE ESTIMATES

Q10

LONG ASHTON COMMUNITY CENTRE
The work will be on Saturdays and Sundays for 7½ hours each day at £3.05 per hour. Applicants sould hold a current driving licence and have the use of a vehicle (mileage paid at a fixed rate).
Although the work is of a 'temporary' nature, Supervisors can expect regular work over an extended period.
WE ARE AN EQUAL OPPORTUNITIES EMPLOYER

Q11

WINDOW PRICES
3 BED SEMI, 8 REPLACEMENT WINDOWS,
DOUBLE GLAZED, FITTED.
10 YEAR GUARANTEE

**uPVC OR   £2544 + V.A.T.
ALUMINIUM
HARDWOOD OR
THERMAL BREAK £2824 + V.A.T.**

*£50 DEPOSIT. BALANCE BUILDING SOCIETY,
FINANCE OR CASH ON COMPLETION*

OPEN 9am-8pm MONDAY-FRIDAY
10am-4pm SATURDAY-SUNDAY

QUALITY AT SENSIBLE PRICES
OVER 2,000 CUSTOMERS, 10 YEARS IN AVON

Q12

UNEMPLOYED
**CALL IN AND SEE US
FOR COLOUR
TELEVISION RENTAL**
£2.60
PER WEEK
NORMALLY 48 HOUR INSTALLATION

C.E.R.   14 High Street
Leyton
Tel: 233496

Q13

TO SUIT ALL MAKES & MODELS!

MINI S/B	£11.50
ALLEGRO 1.1/1.3	£16.70
MAXI 1500/1750	£26.04
MARINA 1.3	£15.60
ITAL 1.3/1.7	£29.50
PRIMERO SFP	£26.90
METRO 900/1600	£27.80
MAESTRO 1.3/1.6 NFP	£32.20
MONTEGO 1.3	£56.50
ACCLAIM	£57.65
ESCORT Mk I/II 1.1/1.3	£17.80
ESCORT Mk III 1.1/1.3 NFP	£27.80
CORTINA 1.6/2.0	£18.20
FIESTA 950/1100	£15.60
CAPRI 1.6/2.0	£24.30
SIERRA 1.3/1.6 NFP	£32.10
ORION 1.3/1.6 NFP	£34.75
ALPINE/SOLARA	£33.00
CHEVETTE	£26.00

MGB
SPECIAL STAINLESS
STEEL OFFER
£74.00
Life Time Guarantee

**ASK FOR DETAILS OF OUR
STAINLESS SYSTEMS —
with Lifetime Guarantees**

Q14

**FILEY
POST OFFICE**

Open 7am - 6.30pm
Mon. - Sat.
Sun. 7.30am - 1.00pm

Q15

Longwell Green

MON & TUES 9 — 5.30
WED & THURS 9 — 8.00
FOR PERMS, HIGHLIGHTS ETC

FRIDAYS 9 — 7.00
FOR CUTS, BLOW DRY ETC

SATURDAYS 9 – 4.00

Q8

Q9

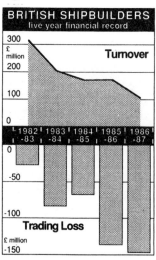

Q10

HOW THEY SPENT ON TV LAST YEAR

	Sponsor	Sport	Hrs/mins	Cost (£)
1	Cornhill	Cricket	189/42	750,000
2	Embassy	Snooker	120/06	350,000
3	Rothmans	Snooker	42/10	275,000
4	Tennents	Snooker	40/05	300,000
5	Benson & Hedges	Snooker	36/50	175,000
6	Mercantile Credit	Snooker	36/10	225,000
7	NatWest	Cricket	36/00	400,000
8	Benson & Hedges	Cricket	31/55	400,000
9	Dulux (ICI)	Snooker	31/50	275,000
10	Texaco	Cricket	31/37	250,000
11	Midland Bank	Bowls	30/20	n/a
12	Bristol Coin Exch	Snooker	28/15	175,000
13	Hofmeister	Snooker	27/15	200,000
14	CIS	Bowls	25/50	30,000
15	Liverpool Victoria	Bowls	19/50	34,000
16	Embassy	Bowls	19/20	131,000
17	Embassy	Darts	17/50	52,500
18	Car Care	Snooker	17/30*	50,000
19	John Player	Cricket	17/25*	73,450
20	Suntory	Golf	17/02	180,000

Q11

Q12

Microcomputer	Number of authorities	Percentage of authorities
None	12	16.67
RML 380-Z	16	22.22
Apple II	30	41.67
Commodore Pet	35	48.61
Sharp MZ-80K	12	16.67
Tandy TRS-80	31	43.06
Acorn Atom	27	37.50
Sinclair ZX-80/81	34	47.22
ITT 2020	7	9.72
Video Genie	6	8.33
Sorcerer	4	5.56
Other	14	19.44

continued ▶

Q13

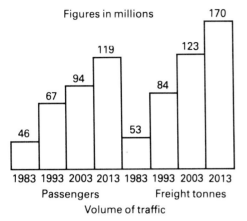

Figures in millions

| | | | | | | | |
|46|67|94|119|53|84|123|170|

1983 1993 2003 2013   1983 1993 2003 2013

Passengers   Freight tonnes

Volume of traffic

Q14

Paperbacks

1	(1)	A Matter of Honour	Jeffrey Archer	Coronet £2.95
2	(—)	Hollywood Husbands	Jackie Collins	Pan £3.50
3	(2)	Act of Will	Barbara Taylor Bradford	Grafton £3.95
4	(4)	Backcloth	Dirk Bogarde	Penguin £3.50
5	(—)	The Mirror of Her Dreams	S Donaldson	Fontana £2.95
6	(5)	The Magic Cottage	James Herbert	NEL £2.95
7	(3)	Power of the Sword	Wilbur Smith	Pan £3.50
8	(—)	Lady of Hay	Barbara Erskine	Sphere £3.95
9	(7)	Dark Angel	Virginia Andrews	Fontana £2.95
10	(6)	The Raven in the Foregate	Ellis Peters	Futura £2.50

Fiction

1	(2)	Dirk Gently's Holistic Detective Agency		
			Douglas Adams	Heinemann £9.95
2	(5)	Sepulchre	James Herbert	Hodder £10.95
3	(3)	Rage	Wilbur Smith	Heinemann £11.95
4	(4)	Sarum	Edward Rutherfurd	Century £9.95
5	(1)	The Songlines	Bruce Chatwin	Cape £10.95
6	(—)	Einstein's Monsters	Martin Amis	Cape £5.95
7	(6)	The Radiant Way	Margaret Drabble	Weidenfeld £10.95
8	(10)	The Eyes of the Dragon	Stephen King	Macdonald £10.95
9	(—)	The Hobbit	J R R Tolkien	Unwin Hyman £7.95
10	(8)	Close Quarters	William Golding	Faber £9.95

General Books

1	(4)	British Hit Singles		
			Paul Gambaccini, Tim Rice & Jo Rice	Guinness £7.95
2	(2)	Boycott: The Autobiography	G Boycott	Macmillan £14.95
3	(2)	Cricket Xxxx Cricket	Frances Edmonds	Kingswood £10.95
4	(3)	Roget's Thesaurus, New Edn	Betty Kirkpatrick	Longman £11.95
5	(—)	Reader's Digest New DIY Manual		Hodder £19.95
6	(—)	Crimewatch UK	Nick Ross & Sue Cook	Hodder £6.95
7	(—)	Complete Cookery Course	Delia Smith	BBC £10.95
8	(6)	The Haw-Lantern	Seamus Heaney	Faber £7.95/3.95
9	(—)	Wainwright's Coast to Coast WalkA Wainwright		M Joseph £13.95
10	(—)	Mediterranean Cookery	Claudia Roden	BBC £12.95

Q15

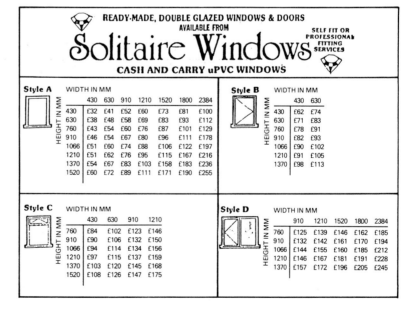

Style A   WIDTH IN MM

HEIGHT IN MM	430	630	910	1210	1520	1800	2384
430	£32	£41	£52	£60	£73	£81	£100
630	£38	£48	£58	£69	£83	£93	£112
760	£43	£54	£60	£76	£87	£101	£129
910	£46	£54	£67	£80	£96	£111	£178
1066	£51	£60	£74	£88	£106	£122	£197
1210	£51	£62	£76	£95	£115	£167	£216
1370	£54	£67	£83	£103	£158	£183	£236
1520	£60	£72	£89	£111	£171	£190	£255

Style B   WIDTH IN MM

HEIGHT IN MM	430	630
430	£62	£74
630	£71	£83
760	£78	£91
910	£82	£93
1066	£90	£102
1210	£91	£105
1370	£98	£113

Style C   WIDTH IN MM

HEIGHT IN MM	430	630	910	1210
760	£84	£102	£123	£146
910	£90	£106	£132	£150
1066	£94	£114	£134	£156
1210	£97	£115	£137	£159
1370	£103	£120	£145	£168
1520	£108	£126	£147	£175

Style D   WIDTH IN MM

HEIGHT IN MM	910	1210	1520	1800	2384
760	£125	£139	£146	£162	£185
910	£132	£142	£161	£170	£194
1066	£144	£155	£160	£185	£212
1210	£146	£167	£181	£191	£228
1370	£157	£172	£196	£205	£245

Q8

Q9

Q10

Census Returns as at 31st March	1985	1986	1987
Beavers	92	159	164
Cub Scouts	708	672	641
Scouts	411	440	413
Venture Scouts	69	73	74
	1,280	1,344	1,292
Instructors	46	42	30
Scouters	154	148	120
Scout Fellowship Members	30	31	24
	1,510	1,565	1,466

Q11

Q12

Q13

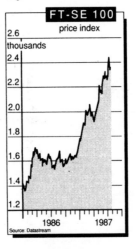

FT-SE 100 price index

Source: Datastream

Q14

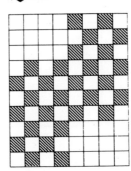

Q15

Qty	Title	Retail £
	Chart 1 (A) – Eastern Channel	6.50
	Chart 2 ★ – Western Channel	5.75
	Chart 3 (A) – The East Coast	6.50
	Chart 4 ★ – Essex Rivers	5.75
	Chart 5 ★ – Thames Estuary	5.75
	Chart 6 – Suffolk Rivers	5.75
	Chart 7 – Central Channel	5.75
	Chart 9 – Goodwins/Selsey Bill	5.75
	Chart 10 – Chichester/Langstone Hbrs	5.75
	Chart 11 ★ – The Solent	5.75
	Chart 12 ★ – Needles/Start Point	5.75
	Chart 13 – Start Point/Lands End	5.75
	Chart 14 – Bristol Channel	5.75
	Chart 15 – Poole/Christchurch Hbrs.	5.75
	Chart 16 (A) – Channel Islands	6.50
	Chart 17 (A) – N. Brittany Coast	6.50
	Chart 19 ★ – Southern North Sea	5.75

(A) – Allweather waterproof chart
★ – Allweather edition due during 1987 @ £6.50

Q8

REGENCY TIMBER SUPPLIES

TIMBER
SCANDINAVIAN PINE

Size	Sawn	Planed
2 x 1	7p per foot	12p per foot
2 x 2	14p per foot	23p per foot
3 x 2	21p per foot	35p per foot
4 x 2	28p per foot	46p per foot

Shiplap Boarding 15p per foot
T&G Matchboard 12p per foot
Full range of exterior quality plywood. i.e. 8'x4' ¼ ply
£8.50 per sheet
8'x4' 18mm chipboard only **£6.98** per sheet

QUALITY SHEDS DIRECT FROM THE MANUFACTURER
Apex or Pent. Shiplap Board Construction
Prices include: Solid timber floor ★ Glass ★ Felt
and Exterior treatment

6'x4' at **£143**   7'x5' at **£160**
8'x6' at **£176**   10'x6' at **£242**

Special sizes made to order
Plus - new solar sheds. Part shed - part greenhouse
from **£280** (6x4)   Free Local Delivery
ALL PRICES SUBJECT TO V.A.T.

4 Ploughmans Way, Carlton
Tel: 761761

Q9

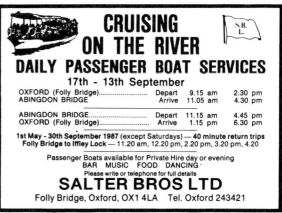

CRUISING ON THE RIVER
DAILY PASSENGER BOAT SERVICES
17th - 13th September

OXFORD (Folly Bridge)	Depart	9.15 am	2.30 pm
ABINGDON BRIDGE	Arrive	11.05 am	4.30 pm
ABINGDON BRIDGE	Depart	11.15 am	4.45 pm
OXFORD (Folly Bridge)	Arrive	1.15 pm	6.30 pm

1st May - 30th September 1987 (except Saturdays) — 40 minute return trips
Folly Bridge to Iffley Lock — 11.20 am, 12.20 pm, 2.20 pm, 3.20 pm, 4.20

Passenger Boats available for Private Hire day or evening
BAR   MUSIC   FOOD   DANCING ·
Please write or telephone for full details
SALTER BROS LTD
Folly Bridge, Oxford, OX1 4LA   Tel. Oxford 243421

Q10

	Originally	NOW
Vi Spring. Pair of 3'3" divans	£2,077.50	**£1,495**
Relyon Braemar 4'6" wide divan set	£799	**£679**
Sleepeezee Backmaster 4'6" wide divan set	£549.95	**£469.95**
Sleepeezee. 3' wide twosome storage bed	£575	**£449**

Q11

GRADE 1 SCHOOL OF MOTORING

£7 Full Hourly Lessons
£3.50 First Lesson
M.O.T. A.D.I. Instructor

Reduced Rates for Block Bookings.

Q12

Q13

LIGHTS

May 6: 9.06 pm to 4.58 am

Q14

ARE YOU THINKING OF EXTENDING YOUR HOME THIS YEAR?

Perhaps you want somewhere to do the ironing, or simply somewhere to just sit and relax? Yes?
Well we can add a brand new dimension to your home in the form of a Conservatory for a lot less than a traditional home extension.
We offer a comprehensive range of services from survey through to installation coupled with very competitive prices. e.g.

Highlight 8 x 10 **£977**,
Garden Room 8 x 10 **£1,119**
Marlborough 8 x 10 **£1,840**
ERECTED INC. V.A.T.
Double glazed from **£3057** and much, much more.
INTERESTED?
Well why not give us a call or visit our large Display Centre at Cadbury Gdn. Centre, Congresbury and choose your Conservatory from our huge range this weekend.

Q15

Spring Genesis Suite
Normally £435 +VAT
3 ONLY £199 +VAT

Acknowledgements

The authors are grateful to the following, who have kindly permitted reproduction of material for the information sheets in this series of books:

Apple Tree Kitchens, Argos Distributors Ltd, Argos Specialist Exhibitions Ltd, Asda Superstores, Automobile Association, B&Q, BP Group of Companies, Badgerline, The Barbican Centre, Barclays Bank plc, Beejam Freezer Food Centres Ltd, Beejay Television, The Boots Co. plc, Bristol 6 Motorcycles, Bristol & West Building Society, Bristol Bus Co., Bristol Channel Cruises Ltd, Bristol City Council, Bristol Rovers Football Club plc, British Airways plc, British Channel Island Ferries, British Rail, The British Shoe Corporation, British Telecom, Brittany Ferries, Broad Finance, Tony Burges, CER, Caldon of Watford Ltd, Camden Graphics Ltd, Camelot Finance, Cannon Cinema, Cheshire Bus, Clevedon Mercury, Co-operative Bank plc, Currys, DSM Finance, Daily Express, Daily Mail, Datastream International Ltd, Department of Education & Science, Department of Transport, East Somerset Railway, Educational Computing, Esso Petroleum Co. Ltd, Evening Post, The Exploratory Hands-on Science Centre, Fuji Photo Film (UK) Ltd, GB Sales and Marketing, Gateway Food Markets, General Accident, The Geographical Magazine, GKN Keller Foundations, Goodwood Travel Ltd, Goodyear Tyre and Rubber Co. Ltd, Granada Group plc, Hanwell Car Centre, David J. Harvey, Hawk Autoparts, Heinz Co. Ltd, Hewitt Ford, Hotpoint Ltd, Hygena, ICC Group, Ideal Homes, The Independent, Kingsdown Sports Centre, Kingston Bagpuize (House & Gardens), Ladbroke Racing, Leos Superstore, Lloyds Bank plc, The London Evening Standard, London Flight Centre, Maitland Finance Ltd, Meat & Livestock Commission, Milk Marketing Board, Money Observer, National Breakdown Service, National Bus Co., National Holidays Ltd, Nationwide Anglia Building Society, New Scientist, The Observer, Olau Line, Oxford Mail, Oxford United Supporters' Club, P&O Down Under Club, Paignton and Dartmouth Steam Railway, Parks Department, Physics Education, Pickfords Removals Ltd, Porsche Cars, Post Office, Quince Honey Farm, RAF Fairford, Radio Times, River Dart Cruises, L. Rose & Co. Ltd, Royal Mail, Royal Yachting Association, Ryvita, Safeway Food Stores, Sainsbury plc, Salter Bros Ltd, Scotcade Ltd, Sealink UK Ltd, Sun Life Assurance Society plc, TNT Overnight Parcels Express Ltd, The Sunday Times, Tesco Stores Ltd, Texas Homecare, Thomson Holidays Ltd, Townsend Thoresen, Train Lines, Transprints (UK) Ltd, TV Times, Unigate plc, Vale of Glamorgan Post, Vauxhall Motors Ltd, Weston and Worle News, Weston Mercury, Weston Super Mare Admag, Which? Magazine, Woman's Realm.

Every effort has been made to contact the sources of the material used on the information sheets, but the publishers will be pleased to rectify any omissions in future printings.